The Secret of Successful
Steeplechasing

The Secret of Successful Steeplechasing

'MOSTLY CHASING, SOMETIMES HUNTING AND A LITTLE DRESSAGE'

TONY PEARN, M.F.H.
(Major R.M., Retd.)
with a Foreword by
FRED WINTER, C.B.E

PELHAM BOOKS

First published in Great Britain by PELHAM BOOKS LTD
52 Bedford Square, London, W.C.1
1972

7207 0584 3

Set and printed in Great Britain by
Tonbridge Printers Ltd, Peach Hall Works, Tonbridge, Kent
in Times eleven on thirteen point on paper supplied by
P. F. Bingham Ltd, and bound by Dorstel Press,
Harlow

To the living
memory of my mother,
who died 7th February, 1972

Contents

Preface

In this book, with great diffidence, I have tried to give guidance to young people who are just starting to train and ride their own horses in hunt races. I wish to thank my friends for their helpful suggestions which I have included in this book. In particular, I would like to thank both my mother and father, without whose financial assistance and encouragement I would not have achieved what limited success I have with my horses.

My father, when stationed in Gibralter, was the leading owner and trainer there in 1931 and 1932 and I was bitten by the racing bug at an early age.

But please do not think that, by writing this book, I am conceited enough to image for one moment that I have anything like the knowledge of successful National Hunt trainers, such as Captain Ryan Price or Fred Winter.

Gosford Lass is, of course, a fictitious horse and any resemblance between her and any past or present 'chaser is purely co-incidental.

Gosford House,
Ottery St Mary,
East Devon

TONY PEARN

Foreword

by

Fred Winter, C.B.E.

I hate all paperwork and do not have time, particularly
since I started training, to read many books, but I must
confess I have been most impressed by this book, written
primarily for the permit holder who owns, trains and rides
his own horses. It is most informative and full of many
practical suggestions.

At the relatively early age of twenty-one, Tony Pearn
first started training on the flat when serving with the
Commandos in Hong Kong in 1946 and it was, in that year,
when celebrating at the Happy Valley racecourse after
training and riding his first double that he met his wife
(see plate 1 page 64). He was first given a permit to train
under National Hunt Rules in the 1955–56 season. He has
learnt a great deal about training since those days, particularly during the two years he was stationed near
Cholderton and regularly rode out before breakfast seven
mornings a week with that exceptionally talented little
trainer, the late Jack Barratt.

The only advice with which I disagree is the lesson he
draws from his experience in the 1957 Grand National that
at Aintree is it necessary to urge one's mount into every
jump. This may be correct for some horses, but certainly
not for all. In fact in that same race, which I won on
Sundew I adopted quite the opposite riding tactics. I sat
quite still and let Sundew 'fiddle' over the big fences on his
own rather than kick him to make him take off early.

As Tony points out in this book, no two horses are the same and there is no short cut to success. This can only be achieved by hard work and very accurate powers of observation, letting no point of detail escape notice.

Tony Pearn is well qualified to write about eventing, having been fortunate enough to be instructed with flat race trainer, Dick Hern, and the 1951 Olympic Three-Day Event possibles when he was working up for the Badminton Horse Trials in which in the cross-country phase, he came fourth out of thirty-nine starters. He has also had plenty of experience to comment on the administration of hunt races, having been Secretary of the East Devon Foxhounds point-to-point for the last three years, and also Secretary of the Hong Kong Services Race Club in 1946 and a Steward of the Marsa Race Club in Malta during 1959.

I think this is an excellent little book, crammed full of really practical advice; I am sure it will be read with enjoyment not only by owner-trainer-riders, but also by all steeplechase enthusiasts. It is a remarkable achievement for Tony, particularly as he never paid more than 500 gns. for any of his horses, other than 'Chamoretta' and 'Tullaherin Lord', to have had a total of twenty horses in training since 1946 and to have only failed to win races with three of them, except the three he bought very cheaply with bad legs, which broke down as soon as they got on a racecourse.

F.T.W.

PART ONE

Practical Advice for the
Owner-Trainer-Rider

CHAPTER ONE

Introduction

My object in writing the following letters which have been collected together to form this book, was to show the best way of getting a horse and rider in the right state of mental and physical fitness so that they can complete a steeplechase course with the maximum speed, jumping ability and endurance combined with the minimum fatigue. The letters cover all the different factors affecting this object. From each factor I have tried to deduce the best practical, and I stress practical, advice for the owner-trainer-rider.

I have four sons, but none of them is called Tom, and these letters have been written for every Tom, every Dick and every Harry, who have ambitions to train and ride winners over fences.

I have always enjoyed reading books about training and riding 'chasers, but all too often they include too much theory and do not get down to the actual practical details which I had hoped to find. I have therefore concentrated as far as I can on practical suggestions with the exception of Chapter Ten, the letter on breeding. I have never had time during my service career to breed for myself and consequently I cannot write from practical experience. But now that I am no longer soldiering, I deeply regret that I sold Chamoretta as she would have been an ideal mare on which to introduce my sons to point-to-point and hunterchase riding, and then I could have bred from her. Out of that great Aintree mare, Tiberetta, I think that Chamoretta is the ideal type of dam to produce a real National sort, and is what I had in mind when writing Part Two of this book, the pipe-dream for Aintree.

When I was riding regularly under N.H. Rules in the late '50s and early '60s, my horses were trained by a number of different professional trainers. I changed trainers often, not because I was dissatisfied, but because I always liked to ride out before breakfast, and consequently, as I was posted from one part of England to another, I engaged a fresh trainer in a different part of the country. I have therefore been able to learn something from each and compare their training methods. The main general difference was their feeding techniques and the amount of exercise they gave each horse. Jack Barratt, for example, had very few facilities at Cholderton and never galloped his horses over a longer distance than about 600 yards, although admittedly one of his longer gallops was up quite a steep slope – yet he was more successful than any of my other trainers, except possibly David Barons who trained for me when I was stationed at Plymouth in 1968.

As an owner-trainer-rider I am convinced that the amount of success you gain will depend on the amount of hard work you put into it, but luck of course plays a big part in racing; however if you are keen you will get an exhilerating feeling of far greater satisfaction if your success is only in an adjacent hunts maiden race, compared with being the owner of a professionally trained horse over the bigger fences. Don't think your geese are swans as Jack Barratt used to say and race them out of their class.

I make no claim to have climbed very far up the ladder of successful training, but I am convinced that methods and techniques expounded in this book are the correct ones.

If I were asked to sum up the secret of successful steeple-chasing in one word, I would without hesitation say 'dedication'. Owners must be dedicated to withstand all the disappointments and financial hazards of chasing, trainers must be dedicated to accept all the worries, disappointments and hard work throughout the coldest months in the year, and riders must be dedicated to compete with all the disappointments and physical hazards of the jumping game. It is not by chance that I mentioned disappointments three times because unless you are proof against disappointment, steeplechasing is not the sport for you.

In the letters which follow I have assumed that my reader, Tom, was lucky enough to have had the opportunity of riding a really good schoolmaster, such as an aged selling 'chaser in his first season point-to-pointing and that by now he has gained experience, has ridden the odd winner at point-to-point meetings and has reached the stage where he wants to graduate to riding hunterchasing under rules. I feel I must at this stage stress to anyone about to buy his first point-to-point horse that it is worse than useless not to get an experienced safe jumper to teach you in your first season. For a novice jockey to start on a maiden horse is truly a case of the 'blind leading the blind'. So until you have gained the necessary experience, I strongly recommend that you should not try to school and race a 'green' horse. You will more than likely have a crashing fall and if it does not shake your nerve, it will almost certainly shake your horse's and possibly ruin his 'chasing career for ever.

SUMMARY

1. Aim of this book.
2. Practical, not theoretical, advice given throughout book.
3. Don't race your horses out of their class.
4. Dedication is an essential quality for success in any activity, but particularly so in steeplechasing with its many hazards and disappointments.

CHAPTER TWO

Buying

Dear Tom,

Thank you for your letter. I am not surprised to learn that you have decided to buy yourself a young horse to replace old Mythlaw for point-to-points, and to school on for hunterchasing. You do not say whether you are thinking of buying an untried four- or five-year-old or whether you intend buying a young hurdler with 'chasing possibilities. Don't rush your fences and buy the first horse you see. Are you going to advertise in *The Sporting Life* and *Horse and Hound* with a view to buying privately, or will you go to Ascot Sales? If there is a useful horse being offered for sale privately or by a reputable dealer, I think I prefer a private sale to buying at an auction because before a private sale you will get the opportunity to see the horse ridden and to ride the animal yourself which is a great help. If, however, you like the description in the catalogue of a horse to be offered at Ascot Sales, try to contact the owner to find out why he is for sale and to arrange to go over and ride him yourself before the day of the Sales.

But don't be too eager to buy; that grand little trainer, Jack Barratt, always used to tell me that there were no friends in racing, and this is never more true than when buying and selling. The integrity of the seller may be beyond criticism in everything else, but when it comes to selling a horse, you are unlikely to get the truth, and certainly not the whole truth.

If you are thinking of buying in Ireland, I strongly

advise you to make your purchase in the spring so that you will have had him in England for twelve months before you ask him to run in hunters' races the following March. It is generally accepted that Irish horses usually lose their form during the first year after they come to England, but that after a year's acclimitization they regain their best form.

However, whether you buy in England or Ireland, there are some general principles which apply to horses at all ages. It is always advisable to have a methodical procedure when you are inspecting a possible buy; this ensures that you don't miss any small faults. It doesn't matter in what sequence you do it, but I usually start with the head, which I consider most important, and work backwards, then downwards (i.e. head, neck, chest, withers, shoulders, elbows, depth through heart, back, quarters, forelegs, knees, pastern, feet, hindlegs and hocks).

I will go through each in detail:

(1) Head. This should be in proportion to his body, the eye should be large and bold, ears alert and not too small which is said to indicate an ungenerous disposition. Lop ears are often a sign of laziness, but usually indicate staying power. Avoid horses with a bump between the eyes as this is a usual sign of stubborness and bad temper, also ones with a parrot-mouth because these will probably develop digestive trouble.

(2) Neck. This should show quality but avoid ewe necks like the plague. As a general rule, the longer the neck the longer the stride.

(3) Chest. I like to see a horse with a broad chest, but don't go to the extreme and buy a horse whose chest is too wide.

(4) Withers and Shoulders. If you can, buy an animal with clean high withers and nice sloping shoulders, which allow plenty of rein. In my opinion there is

21

nothing worse than riding a horse in a race with 'nothing in front of you'.

(5) Elbows. These should be free. This is usually the sign of a good galloper.

(6) Depth through Heart. As you will be looking for a long distance 'chaser, there should be great depth through the heart as this implies staying power.

(7) Back. Don't worry if you find a horse which is a bit long in the back. This, although technically a fault, allows a long swinging stride and plenty of stayers are built this way.

(8) Quarters. I always like to see a bump on the top of the quarters – this is known as a 'Jumper's Bump', and usually indicates a good jumper. But bump or no bump, your horse must have strong quarters.

(9) Forelegs. These should be sturdy and, most important, have not less than eight inches of bone. With less bone than this, horses are unlikely to be able to carry twelve stone seven pounds over three miles at point-to-point speed. You will remember Skara Brae, a nice seven-year-old by Hardraw Scar, who showed plenty of quality, was sixteen hands high, had a bold eye and all the attributes of a very good buy except she only had seven and a half inches of bone. When we had qualified her with the East Devon and were training for the Larkhill point-to-point in February, she broke down and we missed a season's point-to-pointing.

(10) Knees. Beware of horses which are a bit back at the knees. This clearly throws extra strain on the tendons. If you can, go for horses which are a bit over at the knees.

(11) Pastern and Feet. The pastern should neither be too short and upright nor too long and sloping, the former being the indication of a common streak in the horse

22

and the latter a source of weakness. The feet should be examined by looking at the horn; a thick horn being a very much better sign than a thin one; beware of hoofs which are low at the toe and heel as this will almost certainly mean that the hard hoof and soft frog will come to the ground simultaneously which is not a good thing. When the horse is walked towards you, ensure that he doesn't turn his feet out, but preferably turns them in: a great many people are of the opinion that toes turned in slightly indicate speed.

(12) Hindlegs and Hocks. The hocks are most important because it is from here that a 'chaser gets his impulsion for galloping and jumping. Avoid horses with curbs, the bony enlargement at the back of the hock: both point-to-pointers and hunterchasers put tremendous strain on the hocks when jumping.

(13) Colour. The colour of a horse is quite a useful guide. I personally prefer a bay which is a good hard colour and usually a sign of toughness and guts – both most important attributes in a point-to-pointer or hunterchaser. A rich dark brown is definitely my second choice, especially when they have a bold eye. But whatever the horse's colour, it must not be 'washy', by which I mean faded or washed-out in appearance, and this is usually more pronounced on the lower legs towards the feet. Years ago I was taught an old rhyme which ran:

> 'One white foot, buy him,
> Two white feet, try a horse,
> Three white feet, look well about him,
> Four white feet, do without him.'

(14) Sex. A word about the sex of your potential purchase. Mares, especially if well-bred, have the advantage that if they break down and become useless for racing, they still retain some value for breeding purposes.

Against this advantage, it must be pointed out that point-to-points and hunterchases are run in the spring just when mares are coming into season. It is also a fact that, like human females, mares are usually more temperamental than geldings.

(15) Pedigree. Before completing a purchase, have a look at the pedigree. It is a good pointer if the sire of your potential buy is getting winners over three miles, but a number of people think it more important if the dam is a winner herself or has produced winners. I myself think that the dam and sire are equally important and that luck decides which characteristics are passed on to the foal by each parent, but I will go into breeding in more detail in a later letter. If you decide to buy at Ascot Sales, don't forget before the sale to study the breeding in the catalogue of any horse whose description has caught your eye. A little bit of 'classic' blood in a horse's pedigree is a good thing as it usually speeds up the slower staying blood. Also see from the catalogue if your possible buy has any outstanding sires or dams of steeplechasers in his pedigree. I think you may find that Rugantino who was retired to Neville Dent's Shaftesbury Stud a few years ago will soon sire some useful jumpers. Rugantino himself as you probably remember was a very hardy horse and a winner under N.H. Rules.

After a thorough examination of the points I have listed above, have the horse led out and trotted in hand. If he is a good walker he will probably be a good galloper. Look to see if he is a straight mover. After seeing him led out at the walk and trot, see him ridden and carefully note his behaviour, particularly his canter – watch to see if his head is carried lower with a long swinging stride. As I have mentioned earlier in this letter, it does not matter if he turns his toes in when walked and trotted, but he should not produce this defect in his canter. If he does, be very wary about buying him because sooner or later he is certain to knock and lame himself. Then after seeing him led and ridden, ride him yourself. You will remember I said earlier in this letter that there was nothing worse than riding a horse in a race 'with nothing in front of you'. A good sloping shoulder and plenty in front of you is what you are after, but it is much more difficult to judge this from the ground than you would imagine, at least I think it is. For this reason always ride the horse yourself, if possible, before making a buy. Having ridden him, you should be able to decide whether he will suit you or not.

So far in this lengthy letter I have covered the points you must look for when examining a possible buy. But always remember that racehorses win in all shapes and sizes and, as your pocket is not bottomless, you may have to accept a horse which does not conform to all the requirements listed. But whatever you do, don't buy an animal which is not up to a full day's hunting with at least twelve stone on his back when he is being qualified for his hunter's certificate.

That is all for now. Good luck and have fun with your horses.

From,
T.P.

SUMMARY

1. Don't buy in a hurry.
2. Private sale or auction?
3. Irish racehorses need a year to acclimatize.
4. Inspect all points of horse when examining a possible purchase.

5. See him led towards and away from you.
6. Let the sellers ride him first, then if possible ride the horse yourself before making final decision.
7. You are unlikely to find the perfect horse, but don't be disheartened. Horses win in all shapes and sizes.

CHAPTER THREE

Grass and Hunting

Dear Tom,   Overseas

Thank you for your interesting letter about your newly bought five-year-old, Gosford Lass. I was glad to hear that she is a big, strong mare standing about 16.1 hands with a good eight inches of bone. As she has had a few runs over hurdles in Ireland for experience, and already been schooled over regulation fences, you will not have to worry about schooling her to jump. All she will probably need is a few schools 'upsides' another horse over your schooling fences at home before her first race. This will sharpen up her jumping, which she will need after a season hunting with the East Devon where most of the jumping is off the hocks from a slow pace over the Devon banks. I will therefore leave the matter of schooling a young horse now, and cover it fully in later letters (see Chapters 11, 12 and 13).

You can turn Gosford Lass out by the middle of April. As you are not intending to run her in the early National Hunt meetings at Newton Abbot and Haldon next season, I think it best to give her a complete change, leaving her out by day and by night until the beginning of July. If you had wanted to run her in the early West Country meetings in August the best routine would have been to turn her out by day only, as early as possible in May and the first week in June only, giving her a good feed of oats every morning and bring her in at evening stables for the night when she could be given another feed of oats. Of course, if you run her in the August/October meetings she will not under the

27

recent change in the Rules, be eligible to point-to-point next year, but only to hunterchase.

When you turn Gosford Lass out in April, don't think that you can forget all about her. You *must* give her a daily inspection, Particularly if the ground is hard, have a good look at her feet. If you think there is any danger of the walls of her hooves cracking, have short shoes, known as tips, put on around her toes. These should be removed monthly and her toes cut back.

Even though you do not intend to run her in the early meetings, I remember Jack Barratt often telling me that it was advisable to bring thoroughbreds in by day after the 1st July because he considered that by then the goodness had gone out of the grass and also, particularly with thin skinned horses like Le Voyageur, which he trained for me, the flies would worry a horse so much that all the good done by a rest in April, May and June would quickly be undone.

I know you will be keen to hunt her as often as you can in November and December, but at the same time you must give the mare every chance of acquitting herself well in her point-to-points before going on to hunterchases. The secret of this is to bring her in from grass at the beginning of July, and then you can take your time over converting her fat into hard muscle before you ask her to exert herself in the hunting field.

Make sure that the land on which you turn Gosford Lass out, is neither horse-sick nor worm infested. This occurs on land used only for horses for a considerable period of time. Horses are not good grazers; they will only eat the sweeter part of a field, leaving those parts which are coarse to get progressively coarser. One solution to this problem if you are short of grazing is to put a couple of bullocks in the field during the winter months.

Having an expensive thoroughbred at grass is always a worry, but we will assume that all has gone well and that by the beginning of July, Gosford Lass is big and fat. For the first few days in from the grass, it is said to be a good idea to lunge a horse with a saddle on, as this prevents getting sore backs. I have never done it with any of my horses and have never had any trouble with sore backs; but perhaps I have just been lucky.

You must indelibly stamp on the heart of anyone, who is going to help you exercise Gosford Lass during the first three weeks up from grass that 'condition is *walked* on a horse', and make a point of walking Gosford Lass up as many hills as possible. You are lucky at Gosford to have East Hill and West Hill practically on your doorstep. During this period her ration should be steadily increased from four to ten pounds of oats a day, and her hay correspondingly reduced. By the end of the third week she should be able to do some canters and, if brought in in July as I have proposed, she should also be able in late August, go out at hound exercise and start cub-hunting in September. Cub-hunting is, in my opinion, the best possible method of conditioning a horse as it provides much walking, a little trotting and cantering and a very occasional gallop. Generally speaking if you adopt the above outline time-table I have just suggested, you should have the mare in the right condition to stand up to three days hunting a fortnight in November and December which will enable you to qualify her before the New Year.

A few words about hunting. If you don't already know the huntsman's calls, make a point of learning them, also learn the horn notes and their meaning; this will enable you to know exactly what is happening throughout the day's sport. Hunting consists of many pauses, and if you do not understand what you hear you will soon get bored with it. But as you are hunting, not only to qualify Gosford Lass, but also for the fun of hunting, try to make the many pauses as interesting as they can be. Even if no fox has been found, listen to the huntsman's voice and horn signals and you will find that you don't get bored.

Sooner or later you will meet someone who wants to stop

hunting, so let me digress on foxhunting in general. Most people accept that foxes must be controlled, and what are the alternatives to hunting? Snaring, gassing, poison and other fiendish methods are not on, so what are you left with? Shooting? But this is no humane way of killing a fox. Only a few foxes would be killed instantly. And make no mistake, the threat by the 'antis' to your freedom embraces not only hunting, but if ever they succeeded in making hunting illegal, they would soon turn to show jumping, eventing and even steeplechasing. Shortly after I was appointed Joint Master of the East Devon, I received some verses entitled 'The Ballard of the Chase' from an anonymous sender. It contained twenty verses, each of six lines and was signed 'The United Humanitarian League'. The closing two verses were:

'O, slaughterers of England!
O, cowards of the chase!
If you can torture living beings,
And think it no disgrace,
You are a blot upon our land,
A stain upon our race.

Somehow, some day, in some strange way,
We hope it may befall,
You'll have to answer for such deeds,
Unto the Lord of all:
"The Mills of God grind slowly
But they grind exceedingly small." '

My immediate reaction was to think of an ancient verse I learnt years ago:

'Yet if once we efface the joys of the chase,
From the land and outroot the stud,
Goodbye to the Anglo-Saxon race,
Farewell to the Norman blood'!

30

But, seriously Tom, one day you may be confronted by an 'anti' and asked to state the case for foxhunting; I will give you my full answer in a later letter when I have more time (see Chapter 9). We have an excellent case and one which must be put forward with all your forcefulness.

From,

T.P.

SUMMARY

1. All horses at grass *must* be inspected thoroughly each day.
2. Have a look at horse's feet. If necessary have 'tips' put on.
3. Bring horses in by day after end of June because:
   (a) Goodness goes out of grass at beginning of July.
   (b) Flies will irritate horses particularly in July and August.
4. Ensure land is not horse-sick.
5. 'Condition is *walked* on a horse'.
6. After three weeks in from grass horse should be able to have slow canters.
7. Cub-hunting is strongly recommended for conditioning horses.
8. If not hunted, how else can foxes be humanely controlled?

CHAPTER FOUR

Stable Management

Overseas

Dear Tom,

I am glad you will have completed your qualifying before Christmas, as that will give you an opportunity to give Gosford Lass two weeks light work to freshen and build her up before you adopt a proper training routine for her in early January.

It is a good idea as soon as she stops hunting to send a specimen of her droppings to your vet because you don't want to fill Gosford Lass up with oats for the worms to eat, and make sure at this stage that her teeth don't need filing (i.e. see if she has any sharp points or edges).

During her short rest remember to cut her oats. It is better to give her two pounds too few than one pound too many and put her off her feed. If she has had a hard season hunting and is looking a bit tucked up, you must put some flesh on her before you put her into strong work. During the rest period, for her evening feed try the following: Allow two pounds of boiled barley to simmer for at least four hours, then pour three pints of boiling water on to one pound of the seed itself of linseed (not the cake or the meal). Allow this to stand for twenty-four hours. You then have a jelly which you add to the barley with about three-quarters of an ounce of salt. Mix it all up and feed it, but don't give more than one pound every other day or half a pound a day.

And, of course, once you turn your hunting stable into a racing establishment at the beginning of January, it is absolutely essential that you start a regular inflexible routine. This will do a lot to steady her nerves, and she should not only rest better, but also feed better which is all important. I often heard Jack Barratt say that provided an animal in training will eat them, you cannot give her too many of the best possible quality oats, although I know a number of knowledgeable people who say that too many oats will overtax the stomach. I wonder. If the proof of the pudding is in the eating, Jack Barratt certainly trained more than his share of winners. He believed in giving his horses as much as they could eat, and then turning any superfluous flesh into muscle.

Peter Cazalet, the Queen Mother's N.H. trainer, is a firm believer in the dictum that 'races are won in the stables' by which he means that good stable management and the best possible forage are more important than the distances over which a horse is galloped and exercised, though of course it is necessary for a horse to be physically fit before he can go to the post with any expectation of winning. Mr Cazalet told me some years ago that in his opinion racehorses should get their first feed really early before the hurly burly of morning stables distracted them. By adopting this early feed – all his horses are fed before 5.30 a.m. in the jumping season – he can get his horses to feed better and able to digest their feed before they are required to do any fast work.

The ideal stable routine recommended by Mr Cazalet for a chasing stable is as follows, but of course this has to be altered depending on the time of year: At the beginning of training in July the earlier they can be got out the better. In this way they can get their exercise and work before it gets too hot and also avoid the flies. In mid-winter horses cannot get out before 7.30 a.m. when they should require less work and not be out so long.

5.30 a.m. First feed (about two pounds crushed oats and a little bran).

6.30 a.m. Early morning stables (all boxes mucked out, water buckets refilled) first lot prepared for exercise.

7.15 a.m. First lot leave stables.

8.45 a.m. First lot return to stables (ten pounds hay).

9.45 a.m. Second lot leave stables.

11.15 a.m. Second lot return to stables (ten pounds of hay).

11.30 a.m. Tack cleaned, boxes and yard swept.

12.45 p.m. Feed all horses four pounds crushed oats, bran and chaff, plus Mollasine.

4.00 p.m. Afternoon stables. Each horse groomed and strapped for half an hour.

6.00 p.m. Feed six to eight pounds crushed oats, ten pounds hay and chaff and approximately two pounds boiled food, also one to one and a half pounds bran.

Any additives, minerals, vitamins, honey, mollases, etc., should be given in the last feed as most horses are good night feeders. Care should be taken when horses are racing that any stimulants which cannot be classified as food are not given. When horses are in training and looking well, boiled food can be discontinued except for a mash of boiled barley and oats mixed with bran once or twice a week. One to one and a half pounds of damp bran per horse is necesary in the evening feed as a laxative, and as a base in which to mix and absorb the additives. 10.00 p.m. Final look round.

(*Note.* At one time Mr Cazalet thought it a good idea to feed oats and bran with the hay on return to stables after the morning exercise, but this second morning feed was discontinued as it was found some horses would leave part of their midday feed. The quantities stated in the above routine apply to the average good doer but each horse has to be treated as an individual. Shy feeders can be encouraged by various methods but many horses will do and look well on much less than the amounts prescribed.)

The above is a practical routine for a licensed trainer, but, as an owner-trainer with only two horses in training and competent riders available to exercise them together in one lot, I do not think there is any point at all in your starting your stable routine at 5.30 a.m., and I doubt if it will have any adverse affect on your training results if you delay your forenoon stable routine by three hours (i.e. having first feed at 8.30 a.m., and daily exercise in a single lot between 10.15 a.m. and 11.45 a.m.), but whatever routine you adopt you must make certain that you keep to it religiously.

When I was training in Hong Kong in 1946, my Indian head lad, insisted on the chinese *mafoos* (grooms) leading their horses out for twenty minutes walking exercise between the afternoon stables and the evening feed. Since then, whenever I have lived near enough to my trainer's stables, I regularly used to lead my own horses out for about fifteen minutes. It certainly seemed to pay good dividends – the horses obviously enjoyed their afternoon stroll, and only three of the twenty horses, which I have had in training since 1946, have failed to win me a race, except the three cheap buys with bad legs, which broke down as soon as they got on a racecourse, and have taught me it is not worth gambling with unsound horses. The average price I paid was a little over 400 gns. each – by far the most expensive being one of those which did not win! But that is the way luck goes in racing, and I've certainly been damned lucky – a farmer in Wiltshire said to me in 1958, after I had had an unexpected win, that I was so lucky that if I fell into a pond, I would get out dry!

But to return to stable management. Correct feeding and a sensible amount of exercise are the two main pillars on which to build your reputation as a trainer, and grooming and strapping, which I will discuss later in this letter, are the third factor which will ensure physical fitness and this goes hand in glove with mental alertness and contentment, which you achieve by having good roomy boxes, preferably facing south-west, allowing your horses to see each other and, most important, allowing them to rest quietly during the two hours after their midday feed. You must therefore make certain that once you put your horses into training, their bedding must be down before the midday meal so that they can lie down if they wish to do so during their two hours siesta after their feed.

Remember that every horse is a different *individual* and that the rations, on which one horse may thrive, may be not at all suitable for another. As a general rule, I am inclined to recommend that you use bruised oats as opposed to whole ones as they are more easily digested and always remember that the horse's food must be regulated in direct proportion to his work, the more fast work, the more oats required. You know of course that a horse's stomach is very small compared with the size of the horse, and hence the old saying: 'Feed little and often'.

A horse's basic feeds should include oats, bran, linseed, beans and hay, but most trainers like to add their own particular 'special' favourite extras. Above all, get the very best old oats obtainable. It is *useless* trying to lay down standard amounts of oats, bran, hay, etc., which all horses in training should be given, as horses vary a great deal in the amount they will eat when in strong work, but it will probably be something between fourteen and twenty pounds of oats per day. So give Gosford Lass as many oats as she will eat *provided* she eats up her complete feed. You will have to find out by trial and error how much to feed her but as a general guide she should be given very slightly less than she will readily eat.

A double handful of bran in each feed prevents a greedy horse bolting his/her food; thus bran will both help Gosford Lass's digestion and also prevent the loss of part of the nutriment in the oats. Bran is a most important auxiliary because it contains a large proportion of salts, and salt is a valuable aid to digestion. If fed dry it is constipating, if wet it is a mild laxative, the bran mash being an excellent laxative. Coarse salt can also be added to the mash – it flavours it and at the same time provides an essential mineral. Always have a Rock Salt Lick in the loose box. It will also be a good plan to give Gosford Lass a bran mash every Wednesday evening and also on Saturday, but add some boiled linseed to Saturday's mash. Linseed must always be boiled before being fed to horses. Firstly it acts as a laxative and secondly it adds oil to the horse's ration, giving a loose shining coat which is the outward sign of a fit and healthy horse. Barley too is a good body builder, and another useful variation is sugar beet pulp, which has been soaked for twenty-four hours in cold water.

It is said that rye grass and clover from a second year ley is the best hay for a steeplechaser, but I know a trainer with whom I had a horse in training, who thought that Canadian hay was better. I don't claim to know – I have heard so many different opinions – but I think it really boils down to which sort your mare likes best. Regarding the quantity of hay, unless Gosford Lass is a very gross feeder, let her have as much hay as she wants but don't let her eat hay in preference to oats! I think it is a good idea to add two handfuls of chaff with each feed, but remember that a balanced diet is essential and on a ration of oats and hay only you are unlikely to win many races with Gosford Lass.

It is generally considered to be a good thing to mix some beans with the evening feed provided she likes them and is in hard work. Beans are fattening and will heat her blood, so don't give them unless she is in strong work and even then not more than one pound per day. This is quite sufficient.

You should give Gosford Lass some green food. Lucerne, clover, dandelions and green grass should be mixed with her feed and will greatly benefit her digestion and cool her blood. Jack Barratt always used to insist on letting his horse graze for a minute or so at the end of daily exercise before returning to their boxes; he used to tell me that grazing was much better than feeding green food in the stables. Also he always used to add sliced carrots to their feeds, carrots contain vitamin A and are good roughage. But remember that although green foods cool the blood and aid digestion, they are a soft food and must only be fed in small quantities to horses in training. One pound of carrots sliced longways are an excellent addition in winter.

I said earlier in this letter that most trainers have their own favourite special extras to the normal ration. Fred Winter told me that he fed Into View in the 1970–71 season on the same special 'extra' diet as Arkle received in Ireland, namely six raw eggs and two pints of Guinness every day. A good tablespoonful twice a day of demerara sugar is another popular addition. I believe when he was preparing Freddie for the Grand National, Mr Tweedie used to boil a small turnip to shreds and then add it to Freddie's evening mash once a week. This is good for a horse's kidneys.

Some trainers add cod liver oil to malt and feed it as a protection against the cold. This also helps to put on condition and is normally mixed in with the evening mash. I believe a farmer owner-trainer in Cornwall used to give his horses milk to drink instead of water. I was told he thought it was good for their stamina. Another trainer I know likes to give his horses oranges and watercress. I personally like to add glucose to the feed, but two pounds per day is sufficient. Also I like to mix with the oats as many dandelions as I can lay my hands on. Horses appreciate a change in their feed and it encourages them to eat up which is what you want, so also try adding apples, artichokes, potatoes and even sun-dried nettles.

It is a good idea from time to time to place a sod of turf about ten inches by ten inches by two inches thick in the stable at night; you will probably find that it has disappeared by the next morning which is a good sign.

If you can get a regular supply of soft water from a roof water tank, it is better than hard, but if you cannot get soft water regularly, do not alternate from soft to hard. Always keep a bucket of water in each loose box – this is most important.

You may find that once Gosford Lass starts doing fast work she scours. Do not worry about this, but overcome this tendency by a double handful of bran with each feed and reduce her mashes to only one a week. Of course if she is apt to scour, on no account give her any Epsom Salts.

Another point worth considering is having your mangers placed at ground level. After all feeding from the ground is the natural way and it means that the food falls back on to the molars which aids digestive troubles. Also when a horse feeds from the ground, his throat is stretched and open compared with feeding from a manger at the usual height when the neck is bent at a sharp angle in the throat whence comes the 'noise' when a horse has wind trouble.

You must acquire some scales so that you can accurately gauge how many pounds of oats and hay you are giving Gosford Lass, and mark all your measures in pounds for each type of feed they hold when filled to a level top. You seldom see oat-crushing machines, but if you can lay your hands on one, don't hesitate to do so, because once you can bruise your own oats at home when you move them from the granary to the stable bin, but don't bruise more than you require as they keep better unbruised. Incidentally, if you are wondering why I talk about an oat crusher for bruising oats, the only difference between crushing and bruising oats is a different setting on the machine. Another useful piece of equipment is a chaff cutter. So much for feeding, but remember it is the diet that turns out winners.

Grooming, as opposed to strapping, keeps a horse's coat and skin clean, which in turn means that his sweat pores are kept open allowing them to sweat out any waste matter;

start on the near side at the top of the neck with the body brush in the left hand and the curry comb in the right. After grooming her neck and throat, work down to the chest and between the forelegs to the knee. Next, still on the nearside, you do the shoulder, withers, back, loins, flank and under the chest and belly; she may be a little ticklish here and try to cow-kick. You must take great care to remove any sweat marks round the girth, the elbow and where the saddle has been. Next in sequence come the quarters, stifle (around and inside), lifting away the tail between the hindlegs, down to the hock; then repeat the whole thing on the offside, but of course change hands for the body brush and curry comb. After completing both sides, remove his headcollar and do his head, ears, gullet and cheek using the body brush. Then do the legs below the knee using the body brush, or, if the legs are very muddy, the dandy brush being especially careful to ensure that his heels are clean and finally groom his mane and tail with the body brush. After that, take a damp sponge and freshen him up by sponging his nostrils and eyes, and finally with a different sponge, do her dock.

By adopting above routine sequence you will ensure he has been groomed all over, and then finally all you need do is to lift up each of his four feet in turn and thoroughly pick them out.

It is often considered that strapping is an unnecessary luxury which the privately trained horse can do without. I don't subscribe to this theory, though I agree it is not so important as proper feeding and regular exercise. Horses certainly can and do win races with hardly any strapping at all, but if they had had the additional benefit of regular strapping they would probably win more races than they do – rather like a human athlete and massaging. After a good strapping, a horse's blood tingles and he feels very well in himself. You will find also that after his race, he will not be so stiff but recover more quickly due to the strapping. I do not think it necessary to make an old fashioned wisp, and personally I like a larged napkin-sized piece of velvet. Roll it up into a firm ball and do your strapping in a logical sequence, not just in a slap-dash manner. I always start on the nearside at the top of the neck with the velvet pad in my left hand. The velvet should be brought down with the full weight of the body behind it, onto the muscular parts of the horse (i.e. the neck, shoulders, quarters and thighs). It is a good plan to get two people, one strapping each side simultaneously and changing sides every five minutes. By using this method you can get thirty minutes work of strapping in quarter of an hour. It is also more interesting if you strap in conjunction with another person.

If you don't have time to ride out yourself every day, you must make a daily examination of each horse in your charge. You need only spend about two or three minutes with each one. In your daily examination, inspect Gosford Lass carefully all over; if her coat loses its gloss and is staring or dry, and/or if her eye has lost its lustre, then something is wrong and its your job to find the trouble. A staring coat and tight skin probably means worms, so call in your vet, who will arrange for a microscopic examination of a sample of her droppings, and then he will tell you how to get rid of the worms. As well as inspecting the mare, look in her manger to see if she has eaten up and the manger clean. If you find she has left some of her feed, never allow it to remain in the manger which must be cleaned out before the next feed. Look under her rug to make sure she is not losing flesh nor looking tucked up like a greyhound. Don't forget to run your hands very carefully down her legs and around her hooves – heat in her legs is the red warning of trouble ahead. When feeling a horse's legs, my Indian head lad when I was training horses for the flat in Hong Kong in 1946, told me to feel the temperature of a horse's four hooves using the back of your fingers. This, he assured me, would tell me more than passing my hands down his legs, although I must admit I always

41

do the latter. Make certain you look at Gosford Lass's droppings every time you enter her box – you can learn a great deal about her condition from her droppings, they are a sure sign of good or bad health. If her droppings are hard, this indicates over-heating of the blood (you can cure this by putting some bicarbonate of soda in her water), if they are too loose, this means enteritis which is equine diarrhoea. Whole oats in droppings indicate bad digestion. If a horse eats his droppings he needs salt – that is why I advised you earlier in this letter to keep a salt lick permanently on the stable wall.

Well that is a pretty lengthy detailed letter but I wanted to cover the subject as comprehensively as I could as good stable management is of prime importance.

From,

T.P.

SUMMARY

1. Send droppings to the vet, and inspect horse's teeth when brought in from grass.
2. Give boiled feed every day for first fortnight.
3. Turn hunting stables into racing establishment in January.
4. A regular routine is essential for best results.
5. Races are won in the stables.
6. Give horses two quiet hours resting each afternoon.
7. Have salt lick in each loose box.
8. Special 'extra' include carrots, Guinness, raw eggs, apples, oranges, artichokes, potatoes, cod liver oil, glucose and even sun-dried nettles.

9. Groom and strap each horse for half an hour at evening stables.
10. Inspect each horse every day for at least two or three minutes.
11. Look at horses droppings whenever you enter the loose box.

CHAPTER FIVE

Training (Exercise)

January
Overseas

Dear Tom,

I am assuming that you have sent a specimen of Gosford Lass's droppings to your vet and have had a satisfactory report from him, also that you have ascertained that her teeth do not need filing. You are now ready to start your eight weeks training programme during which time you must convert her from hunting fit (stamina) to racing fit (jumping muscles, speed, wind and stamina). As I wrote in my last letter on feeding, you should give her a rest for about two weeks during which time you must build her up before the strenuous fifteen weeks in front of her. Having put some more flesh on her, you must then turn it into muscle concentrating on developing those muscles connected with speed and jumping, and finally you have to clear her windpipes.

Your first stage therefore involves cutting down her exercise to no more than one and a quarter hours per day slow walk (remember condition is *walked* on a horse), and at the same time slightly reduce her oats, but add to her feed-table some beet pulp soaked for twenty-four hours in cold water and mix these with her oats. Also give her three boiled feeds a week with a little linseed and barley. After two weeks Gosford Lass should have put on enough flesh with which to develop her speed muscles by starting her fast work. The amount of work to give Gosford Lass cannot be laid down, you can only find out by trial and error. Horses need different amounts, some need more and

44

some less but remember it is far better to arrive on the point-to-point course with your horse short of a gallop than with her over-galloped. If you are training an excitable animal, she is likely to hot up and go off her feed which is the last thing you want to happen. Usually if horses are placid and good doers, they can have a greater amount of fastwork without any risk of going off their feed and getting tucked up like a greyhound.

Incidentally, and this was a point about which Jack Barratt was very particular; immediately before actually galloping horses 'pick them up' and jump them off straight into a gallop. He had of course always given them a preliminary canter. On completion of the gallop he would always pull them up very gradually into a canter, then a trot, then a walk until finally halting them and making them stand still while he inspected them to see how hard they were blowing.

But to return to Gosford Lass. She is, from all accounts, a good doer and has a placid temperament so after the first fortnight increase her oats again and take her out for two hours, cantering her every day, preferably uphill for about half a mile, and twice a week give her a half speed gallop, but walk for the remainder of her two hours exercise period. Remember all fast work must be done in company with another horse, unless you are training a highly strung animal in which case you may find it better to always exercise her on her own to avoid getting her worked up into a muck sweat. In the case of Gosford Lass, as she is placid, work her in company and always warm her muscles up with a fast trot or, better, a short slow canter before you give her any fast work.

If you can find a suitable uphill gallop, 600 yards is enough; it will reduce the risk of damaging her legs, but don't let her get bored by always using the same gallop. I know David Barons attributes a part of his success to having gallops on all four sides of his stables on his farm near Kingsbridge. Try to arrange with the various farmers around Gosford House to let you use their land for gallops, so that Gosford Lass can have a variety of different gallops – there is one particularly good gallop near Tidwell House just East of Budleigh Salterton, where I used to gallop Tullaherin Lord in the early 1960s. If you have a very cold January and February and the ground is frozen, you are lucky having Exmouth relatively close because if you go on the beach at low water you can ride around the headland at the East and you come to Sandy Bay where you can have a fine gallop, and while you are there let your horses paddle in the salt water because this is very good for their legs. I suggest you contact a friendly farmer and ask him if you may gallop two horses for two miles around his twenty acre field on the Saturday before the mare's first point-to-point race.

Assuming all goes well from the end of the second till the seventh week of your training programme, you now have one final week to finish off Gosford Lass's preparation before her first race. Give her a couple of three-quarter speed gallops, in company of course, but never let her off the bit nor start 'scrubbing' her. As I have said before, try to get uphill gallops to reduce the strain on her legs, and as most point-to-point courses include a downhill stretch, it is not a bad idea to teach your mare to gallop downhill, but don't overdo this. I am always worried about their legs when galloping a horse downhill.

I do not like the habit among some trainers of only clipping trace high. I know that plenty of horses, clipped this way, do win races and I think it quite a good idea while you are qualifying Gosford Lass during November and December, as it will help to keep her warm during the inevitable pauses during a day's hunting; but once you adopt a race trainer's routine in January, clip her all over and continue clipping through the remainder of the winter. When Gosford Lass is in training proper, by all means keep her warm by exercising her in a small blanket over her back and loins. But surely a horse must race better if

46

she is clipped all over. After all a human running a half mile or mile race doesn't wear a sleeveless sweater – they soon get warm once the race starts! I know because in my younger days I was a long distance runner. In fact I am sure that the principles I adopted when training myself for long distance races are the same as those which achieve the best results with a three miles 'chaser.

One final point, although the mare will have to carry twelve stone seven pounds (and twelve stone once she graduates to open races), it is a great mistake to think that you should gallop her, including her two miles three-quarter speed gallop a week before her first race, with this weight on her back – if you do you are taking an unjustifiable risk with her legs.

From,

T.P.

P.S.

Perhaps I should have commenced this letter by defining what is meant when steeplechase trainers refer to the various paces. The canter in a racing stables is not a canter at all but the term used when the horse is galloping a great deal below his racing pace. By a three-quarter speed gallop they mean that the horse is extended but kept down to pace below his best speed, and by a fast gallop they mean that the horse is allowed to gallop at his fastest over a short distance.

SUMMARY

1. Start by sending a vet a specimen of droppings.
2. Ensure teeth are in good order.
3. Give two weeks easy period after qualifying.

4. Give three boiled feeds a week to put on flesh.
5. Under-gallop rather than over-gallop.
6. When training jump horses off straight into gallop after preliminary slow canter.
7. Vary your gallops to avoid staleness.
8. Six hundred yards uphill is long enough.
9. Sea water is good for horses' legs.
10. Give two three-quarter speed gallops in company during final week.
11. Keep horse warm with exercise blanket for slow work.
12. Definitions of 'canter' and 'gallop' when referred to in a racing stables.

CHAPTER SIX

Veterinary Aspects

Dear Tom,   Overseas

I am going to devote this letter to first aid for horses, but remember a little knowledge is dangerous and for goodness sake if you are unfortunate enough to have an unsound horse, do not treat her complaint yourself but send for the vet, and there is no point in paying for his advice if you do not apply the treatment he recommends. Concerning soundness, the three greatest worries in a trainer's life are colds, coughs and bad legs, so I will deal with these first.

If your mare gets a cold, knock her off all fast work and, instead of her evening feed, give her a mash. It is also an old fashioned treatment, but none the less, effective to hold her head two or three times a day over a bucket in which you have put a little hay, some drops of eucalyptus and a kettle of boiling water. If she is quiet a rug should be thrown over her head so that none of the steam escapes. For coughs, the treatment is much the same as for colds. Keep her in a box and let her have hot mashes and extra rugs to keep her warm. If she has a temperature on no account allow her to leave her box and if you have an 'isolation' box away from the others, put her in this as it will help prevent an epidemic from spreading throughout the stables. When she is recovering, if after a steady canter she does not cough, it is a good indication that she is fit to resume work again. Don't worry if she merely 'blows her nose'.

I am a great believer in fresh air and would rather put an extra rug on and leave the top half of her stable open except on the very coldest nights in the year. But *never* allow your mare to stand in a draught. This can be avoided by lowering a rolled up piece of hessian over the top of the stable door. The hessian allows fresh air in, but reduces the risk of a draught. I am sure that fresh air more than anything else keeps a horse fit and free from colds. I personally hate sleeping in a room with the bedroom window closed, and I feel much better if I have an extra blanket on the bed and keep the window open: I believe the same applies to horses.

You will find that horses often blow their nostrils once or twice when they go out in the morning but this is nothing to worry about, however beware of a running nostril as this is a sign of a cold, or worse, of sinus trouble.

Neither a cold nor a cough is nearly so serious as the third worry, bad legs. If a tendon or ligament gives way, a horse is said to have 'broken down'. This can be caused by a variety of different things, but it happens far more often on the racecourse than in the hunting field, which reinforces the claim that it is the 'pace which kills'. Experience has shown that a break down is more likely to occur towards the end of a race when the muscles are tired. Generally speaking, the observant trainer is given a warning by feeling heat in the tendon, during the animal's preparation for the race, and if no heed is paid to this warning then a break down is the likely result. The lesson is 'never work a horse until the heat has gone, and even then only start gradually'. Immediately you diagnose a sprained tendon or ligament, stop all work unless the animal walks sound in which case she may be given walking exercise only, and preferably being led to avoid any weight on her back. For at least ten to fourteen days keep a Kaolin poultice on the leg throughout the twenty-four hours. When you take off the last poultice if the heat and swelling have gone, pick up the foot and bend the knee, then squeeze the injured place between your fingers and thumb and if the horse does not flinch you can consider the animal cured. But it is always as well to have your diagnosis confirmed by your vet. He may recommend you continue treatment for anything up to six weeks; if he does, follow his advice as this may well save you having to blister, or even fire, the horse at a later date if you are too impatient in the early stages of the leg trouble.

My present vet refuses to fire a horse; he says it is an old-fashioned and uncivilized treatment, and that it is poor medicine to heal one injury by inflicting another, and he prefers electrical heat equipment. Personally, I have yet to be convinced that electrical heat equipment is preferable to the old-fashioned method of firing for a permanent cure; of course no vet will fire until the heat and pain has gone out of the tendon. If a vet uses a local anaesthetic he can carry out the whole 'operation' without even having to cast the horse. I think line firing best for tendons, but have often been told by experienced and knowledgeable people that needle firing is better for a sprained suspensory ligament. One big advantage of firing over other methods of treatment is that, after firing, a horse has to be rested for a long time and there is not temptation to put him back into training too soon.

If after a race or fast work one of Gosford Lass's legs is suspect, wrap a hot water bandage, soaked in vinegar, loosely round the leg and cover it with polythene to keep the heat in, then secure it with a second bandage.

Many owner-trainers have to train horses with doubtful legs. If you are faced with this problem, give your horse as much road work as possible and plenty of time to harden his legs before doing any fast work; it is also a wise plan to keep doubtful legged horses on the lean side. Avoid at all costs sticky going as my experience has been that this is far more likely to cause leg troubles than when the going is on the firm side.

An over-reach is one of the injuries with which you are

most likely to be concerned, particularly if your gallops are very wet and the going heavy, or if you school when the ground is soft. The obvious answer is, of course, to neither gallop nor school in heavy going, but this is not always possible for the owner-trainer of point-to-pointers and hunterchasers, because the hunter race season begins in February and March, often after the wettest two months in the year. It is therefore advisable to take precautions to prevent over-reach by using tendon boots and bandages and, particularly for schooling, I always think it a wise precaution to put rubber over-reach boots on horses. If, however, despite your precautions, you are unlucky enough to have to deal with an over-reach on the bulbs of the heel or back of the fetlock, immediately you return to stables you should thoroughly clean the wound with a hose-pipe, and then put on a bandage with a mild antiseptic lotion. After two days you can usually apply a dry dressing in place of the bandage. If the overhanging lip has to be cut off, this can easily be done using a sharp pair of scissors. If it is a severe over-reach, especially when it concerns the back of the tendon, send for a vet at once.

If Gosford Lass gets sick or injured and has to stay in her box, reduce her feed of oats but continue to groom and strap her as if she was in work. The massaging will have the effect of keeping her muscles firm so that when she re-starts work, her enforced rest will not have put her back so much.

Finally make sure your farrier avoids leaving her toes too long, but don't let him lower the heels too much either as this causes extra strain on the tendons and suspensory ligaments.

That is enough about the gloomy subject of injuries, I think.

From,

T.P.

until the last possible minute, because once Gosford Lass realises this, she will start using up nervous energy; also you may find that she won't eat anything, but better not to eat anything than to race on a belly full of hay! To avoid giving the game away, leave the plaitting of her mane and, if you are good at it, her tail until the last convenient moment before she leaves her box. Also, if you decide to use bandages in the race, put them on in her loose box just before you leave for the course.

I always cut out all hay on the day of the race, and considerably reduce the hay ration on the night before, ensuring that the bedding is of sawdust because a meal of straw bedding during the night will undo all your hard work during the previous two or three weeks.

If you have a suitable gallop near your stable, such as the 'football' field opposite Gosford House, I recommend as a final pipe-opener about a quarter of a mile fast gallop, preferably up a slight slope, before breakfast on the morning of the race, but do not worry unduly if this is not possible due to the ground being too wet or for any other reason because you will in any case be cantering her down to the start before the race which will help clear her pipes; if you cannot gallop her at home it should be a regular routine that you always lead her out, or better, if you yourself are riding her in the race, ride her out for about a quarter of an hour. You will find that this gives both you and your mount mutual confidence. If you have to walk her instead of giving her an early morning pipe-opener, do it *after* her morning feed, or if you are galloping, do it before the morning feed, but either way try to give her her morning feed at the usual time.

Don't let her drink anything after five hours before her race except for a *short* drink about two hours before it. Try to persuade her to eat a good meal of oats mixed with an extra quantity of glucose *not less than* three hours before her race. I realise this may mean stopping on the journey if you are travelling far, but that cannot be helped – in fact, it is very seldom that you will travel more than three hours on the morning of the race; if this looks likely always try to reserve some stabling nearer the course, if not at the course, the latter being the better plan.

Assuming that you are travelling on the day of the race, as soon as you reach the course make sure that she has travelled without mishap, and then leave her to rest quietly in her box. I always like to lead my horse around for about fifteen minutes before any racing begins or, if you are in a late race, between races but *not* during a race as the excitment will communicate itself to her with the consequent loss of nervous energy. After she has stretched her legs, put her back in the box and leave her until after you have weighed out, assuming you are riding her yourself. If possible, weigh out, *before* the preceding race (i.e. as soon as the preceding race riders have weighed out, not weighed in), you can then saddle the mare up in her box, and allow her a good half hour to be led around to brace herself for her race, but don't lead her about actually *during* the race before yours unless you have discovered from experience that the shouting and general excitement does not worry her.

I was given a useful tip by a Maltese groom when I was riding on the flat in Malta in 1959. He told me that if you have difficulty in tightening the girth to the next hole, put the end of the girth leather between your teeth and simultaneously as you pull up with your arms, you also pull upwards on the end with your teeth by forcing your head upwards and backwards. You will find that by using this method you can usually tighten the girth nearly an extra quarter of an inch allowing you to get the girth into the next hole.

After the race, dry her off before you depart for home. It is a good plan to give her a bucket full of water with two pounds of glucose in it as this has the effect of stopping her breaking out both on the journey home and during the night. As soon as you get Gosford Lass home giver her a bucket of chilled linseed water followed by her normal mash.

I think I have covered all the main points which need attention on the day of the race, but if I think of any more, I will send you a further note.

From,

T.P.

SUMMARY

1. Before the Race Day
   (a) Let the saddler check all saddlery
   (b) Give a weekly injection of 10ccs of Vitamin B12
   (c) Arrange for farrier to shoe horse in the afternoon before the race
2. On the Race Day:
   (a) Give no hay on day of race
   (b) Last long drink five hours before race
   (c) Last feed with glucose added three hours before race
   (d) On arrival at the course let the horse stretch her legs
   (e) Weigh out in good time
   (f) After race, give horse a bucket full of water with two pounds of glucose in it
   (g) On arrival home, give horse a bucket full of chilled linseed water, followed by her normal mash

CHAPTER EIGHT

Race Riding

Dear Tom,

One of the best ways of developing a good racing seat is to watch top class professional jockeys like Bob Davies. The more you watch the experts, the more you will unconsciously find that you copy their style. Go down to the start and see how they shorten their reins in a quick movement as the tapes go up, and watch them particularly closely landing over the last, noting how quickly they 'pick up their horses' thus giving their mounts the signal that a final all-out effort is required of them. And watch the take off side, especially at the open ditch, to see how they let the reins slide through their fingers.

To get down to practical details. First of all I hope it is not necessary for me to remind you that you must be as fit as your horse. Except when you are riding your horse into a jump or riding a hard finish, your thigh muscles must be strong enough to enable you to keep the upper part of the thigh and seat out of the saddle from start to finish, the grip being maintained by your knees and lower part of your thighs. It is a horrible sight, seen at some point-to-points where the rider's seat bumps up and down on the saddle. Except at the jumps 'sit' as far forward in the saddle as you can with comfort. Have your foot on the *inside* of the irons. I know that this advice will be frowned upon by many accomplished horsemen, including my father, but I maintain that, *for steeplechasing*, it is better to have your feet on the inside of the iron, because with it here, when you press down on your instep, you will find that your knee and lower thighs are automatically forced closer into the saddle, thus ensuring a tighter grip. To develop my thigh and riding muscles ready for my first race of the season, I have always found it a great help to adopt the 'galloping' position whenever my mount did road work at the trot. By preventing my seat from touching the saddle at the trot (without pulling my seat out of the saddle by *hauling* on his mouth), I found this exercise very beneficial. I suggest you start off this human muscle building exercise by trotting like this initially for say fifty strides, and gradually increase the number until you find you can keep your seat out of the saddle indefinitely without undue fatigue. But don't cheat by standing up in the stirrups, the correct angle at the knee between the shin and the thigh bones should be slightly more than 90 degrees – just enough to keep your seat out of the saddle. If your mount is not pulling, there is no requirement for your lower leg to be forward of the perpendicular. Of course, your shoulder and arm muscles must be fit and strong - probably best achieved by doing pull-ups on any convenient horizontal bar or ledge on which you can get a grip.

So much for your muscles, and don't forget not only your horse's windpipes must be clear, but yours as well. Play plenty of squash or go for a series of short sprints until your wind is fully fit. Race riding is a very tiring business, especially if you are on a lazy horse which has to be kicked all the way in a three mile chase. As a general principle, I would say that the shorter you ride within reason the easier you will find it to keep your feet in the irons, although of course this advantage must be weighed against the disadvantage of keeping your mount properly balanced when you are riding with your leathers too short. You will also find that you can control Gosford Lass better with shorter leathers when galloping, because when she takes a hold, particularly going down to the start, you can 'lean against' her and have much more control than when riding 'long'.

Incidentally, if you are riding a confirmed puller, try using a drop noseband. This will keep the horse's mouth shut, and very often make an uncontrollable horse quite easy to hold. It is also a good idea when saddling before a race to twist the nearside leather clockwise, when looking upwards at the base of the iron, and the offside leather anti-clockwise, so that the irons hang at a right angel to the horse's flanks instead of parallel to them. This makes it easier, if you lose your irons during a race, to regain them. But if you lose an iron and have not regained it by the time you reach the next jump, kick the other foot out, as it is much easier to ride over a jump with no irons, rather than be lopsided with one foot in and the other out.

Before the start of any race, always check your girth yourself and then tighten it if necessary. If your horse 'blows himself out' when being saddled – and a number do – the canter down to the start will make it apparent that the girths should be tightened a hole or two. To get a good start, lean slightly forward with your weight off his hindlegs, and most important of all, watch the starter's *eyes*. No one can drop a flag without giving a split second warning with his eyes – try it yourself if you don't believe me – and it is in that split second that you pick up the reins and urge your mount forward with your legs, thus getting a 'flying start'. Also try to get started on the correct leg (i.e. on the near fore for a left handed course and the off fore for a right handed one). If she makes a bad mistake at a fence let her recover from her blunder before you make up the ground lost, and never try to make up ground going up hill, on the contrary, this is when you should ease her and try to give her a breather. On the other hand, you can urge your mount on when you come to downhill slopes like the one at Larkhill. If you have ever done any cross country running yourself, you will know that it is no more exhausting to speed up going downhill than it is to run slowly.

If Gosford Lass turns out to be a bit one-paced like Mythlaw, you cannot afford to be too far behind the leaders when you are a couple of fences from home because Gosford Lass won't be able to accelerate to catch them on the run in. It is a great mistake with any horse to give him too much to do in the closing stages of a race.

As Gosford Lass is still an inexperienced racehorse, especially during her first few races, don't be half a length behind another horse at the moment of taking off because this will tend to make Gosford Lass take-off simultaneously which, particularly if the other horse stands well back, may be disastrous to her. Some people advocate stopping a horse taking off too soon by riding him into the fence on the bit and not slipping the reins until you are airborne.

If you find that you and, more important, Gosford Lass are blinded as you approach a fence, pull to one side or the other, or if this is not possible, pull her back to give her a better chance of seeing the fence. In her early races the most important thing is to let her see her fences properly; don't get tucked in behind another horse. In her first race over fences she will almost certainly be excited and try to rush at her first few fences completely unbalanced like a bat out of hell, so let her have at least six good strides to see the jump and measure her take-off. Pick easy races to start off with; you may be lucky and win a race early in the point-to-point season which will encourage Gosford Lass to enjoy her racing and become all the more confident. And now a word about your seat when riding in hunterchases over the bigger National Hunt regulation fences. If you adopt the forward seat and Gosford Lass pecks on landing, or takes off too close to the fence and crashes through it, reducing speed from thirty to fifteen mph, unless you take some avoiding action, you will almost certainly be catapulted over her head. For point-to-pointing *on a good jumper* a sensible forward seat is good, but even over the smaller point-to-point fences always take the precaution of letting your lower legs go slight forward – just in case Gosford Lass pecks on landing (see plate 2 page 64). But when riding 'under rules' over the stiffer fences, and indeed in point-to points on a chancy jumper, my advice to you is to try to forget all you have been taught about leaning the body forward when jumping, but instead learn to straighten the body slightly as Gosford Lass jumps over the fence, at the same time, if necessary, slipping the reins a little to give her the full freedom of her neck and head, but maintaining the lightest contact with her mouth, and also let your legs go slightly forward. If you see that she is meeting a fence all wrong and it is too late to ask her to stand back, there is precious little you can do except let your reins slip to the buckle and 'give her the lot', simultaneously leaning back and putting your legs forward as you would do in the front passenger seat in a car which is about to crash. (See plate 3 page 64.) It may not look so elegant as the forward seat, but it is very much more effective on a doubtful jumper! I have read articles by knowledgeable writers saying that when steeplechasing sitting upright and slipping the reins through the hands is a sign of bad horsemanship. I disagree: the crucial test is to watch whether the horse's mouth is open or not: if it is open it means that the rider has got left behind and is clinging on by the reins, but if the horse has his mouth shut, it means that the rider has not been left behind but has simply taken the precaution of straightening his body which will sooner or later prevent him from being unseated. When you are a maestro like Fred Winter, you will know when it is safe to adopt a forward seat and when it is not. But until you have far more experience it is better to be safe than sorry so straighten your body slightly, slip the reins if necessary and allow your legs to go a little forward. I have very small hands and always found it difficult to slip rubber covered racing reins through my fingers (see plate 4 page 64). In fact when I rode in the 1957 Grand National I had specially narrow reins made with rubber only on one side to make it easier for me to slip the reins on landing over Bechers Brook – and I didn't get unseated at Bechers! – to be honest, I did not get that far!!

If you are riding a very good experienced jumper, all you need do on a park course to give him the extra rein he requires, is to straighten your arms at the elbows without slipping the reins at all. Always ride with your reins forming a 'bridge' between your hands.

Don't be careless about jumping the last jump, especially if you happen to be in front and clear of the rest of the field – sit down and ride Gosford Lass into it (i.e. squeeze your horse with your lower legs, pushing forward on the saddle with your seat bones and back muscles in rhythmn with the horse's final few strides before taking off; by pushing forward with your seat bones I mean much the same action as you used to push a swing forward with your seat when you were young.) It is imperative to ride with the same determination as you have shown at the earlier jumps – remember careless riding breeds careless jumping.

There is an old proverb which says that it is not enough to learn how to stay in the saddle, a jockey must also learn how to fall! (See plate 7 page 64.) Try to relax your muscles as you feel yourself being catapaulted from your horse and it is safer if you tuck your head into your chest and protect your front by raising your arms together in front of your tucked in head. If you are unlucky and have a fall, lie absolutely still until the rest of the field has passed. I am told that a thoroughbred will not tread nor roll on a man if he can possibly avoid it, but he may kick at a moving object: moral, lie still. Also always make certain you are wearing a regulation helmet, and wear the new plastic backguard which may well save you a long period in hospital.

Plan your riding tactics beforehand. Find out if any of the fancied horses in your race have any characteristics which you can turn to your advantage. Some horses prefer a slow run race and rely on their finishing speed, others do better if a fast pace is set from the beginning. Some tend to jump a bit sketchily if they are hard pressed when tiring at the end of a race; for example, in the 1956 Grand Military Gold Cup, I knew that the favourite Cottage Lace tended to blunder at the last fence if she was hustled at this stage in the race. I therefore determined to try if possible to be up with her over the last two fences, and to drive my horse, Waking, who was a superb jumper, into the last two fences as hard as I could. In the event everything went according to plan and Waking and Cottage Lace jumped the last 'upsides', but unfortunately Cottage Lace failed to oblige on this occasion and instead of blundering as was her habit at this stage, she jumped it very well and her faster speed on the flat gave her owner, Major David Gibson, a well deserved victory (see plate 8 page 65).

During the race, if you see another horse jump to his left, see that you are on his right and *vice versa*. Avoid being on the outside of a hard puller going round a bend because he may run wide and carry you out with him. Do not continually fight with a hard pulling horse, this will waste both his energy and yours, but let him go his own speed for a bit and then as he settles down, ease him and you will find that he will go at the pace you want. Of course, if you are riding someone else's horse and your riding instructions are not to make the running, then you must disregard my advice above as you will be expected to hold him up from the start. If you know you cannot hold a horse try using a drop noseband as this often gives you back complete control.

And now the finish. Until you have had a great deal more experience race riding, I strongly advise you to ride a finish with your hands, legs, seat bones and back muscles and forget all about the whip, except possible a tap on Gosford Lass's shoulder, only whatever you do, avoid unbalancing her in this critical stage of a race. Incidentally 'riding out' with hands (i.e. 'scrubbing') does not simply

The author started training in Hong Kong in 1946 (see page 13). This photo shows the author being led in by his fiancée, Miss Heather Gillespie, after winning the United Services Cup at the Happy Valley Race Course, Hong Kong

The Race Course Security Identity Card of
the author, Major A. W. C. Pearn R.M.
(Retd), M.F.H.

If a horse crashes through a fence and blunders badly on landing, there
is nothing much the rider can do except to 'give his mount the lot!' (see
page 62). This photo shows Vivace blundering badly at the first fence at
Cowdray Park in 1968, and the author 'giving Vicace the lot'. She recovered
and went on to win the Cowdray Cup

When the author started Steeple-chase riding he used to find it difficult to slip his reins through his fingers. Note that horse's mouth is slightly open (see page 62). The photo shows Forest Lad, ridden by the author, jumping the last fence to win the Foxhunter's Cup at the West Street Point-to-Point, 1953. This is not an example to follow. Learn to slip the reins as you straighten your back. (See picture below)

This is a perfect example of the rider (No. 33) allowing the reins to slip through his hands if the horse pecks on landing. This photo was taken at Bechers in the Grand National, 1969

Even over point-to-point fences always take the precaution of letting your leg go slightly forward (see page 62). The author on Camille, taking the fourteenth fence in the East Devon Hunt Member's Race, 1955. They went on to win comfortably

A jockey must learn how to fall if he is to survive long (see page 63). Here the author is being unseated after Skate Up had blundered at the last in the Grand Military Gold Cup, 1964

If a rival horse has a tendency to jump sketchily when he is tiring, try to force the pace into the last jump (see page 64). Here, Waking, ridden by the author (nearest the camera), is jumping alongside Cottage Lace (Maj. D. Gibson) in the Grand Military Gold Cup, 1956. Cottage Lace went on to win with Waking second

To become a clever jumper, a horse needs all the jumping experience he can gain, both out hunting and in cross-country competitions (see page 94). Here the author is seen on Bambridge Boy over one of the jumps in the cross-country phase of the Badminton Horse Trials, 1951. Bambridge Boy was placed fourth in the cross-country phase

The author is a strong believer in 'horses for courses' (see page 109). Here he is riding Waking at the last fence at Plumpton to win the Lewes Handicap Chase in 1957. Waking always ran a good race at Plumpton. This win gave the author and his trainer Jack Barratt, the second leg of a 100-6 (Happy Slave) and 100-8 (Waking) double that day at Plumpton

The first fence is never the happiest stage in a race (see page 116). The author can just be seen (fifth from the left) galloping away on Waking after landing safely over the first fence in the 1957 Grand National

'Don't look down or you will get giddy and fall off!' (see page 113). A worm's eye view of the horses going over Bechers in the 1969 Grand National.

mean pushing with the bridge of the reins on her neck, but also maintaining contact with her mouth by bending your wrists and moving your hands backwards and forwards in time with her strides. Keep your elbows in – there is nothing more unsightly than seeing an amateur, or a professional for that matter, riding a finish with his elbows and arms flapping about from side to side. And finally do not forget to urge your mount forward with your voice. This is a very useful aid, or perhaps do what a Chinese trainer in Hong Kong told me to do – hiss through your teeth.

You never stop learning about race riding so don't think, because you have had moderate success on aged safe jumpers, that you know it all, you don't. If you take the trouble you can learn something new from practically every race you ride in, especially when you are riding different horses.

In the same way that a frightened rider conveys his fear to a horse, so does a determined rider convey his determination, so always race ride with an unyielding will to win.

From,

T.P.

SUMMARY

1. Take every opportunity to watch top-class jockeys in action.
2. Get yourself fit.
3. Press down on the inside of the irons to ensure a tighter grip of the saddle.
4. Riding exercises for the rider.
5. Watch the starter's eyes.
6. Start on the correct leg.

7. Don't make up lost ground in a hurry.
8. Don't push your horse going uphill.
9. Don't give your horse too much to do in the closing stages of a race.
10. Don't get half-lengthened at the jumps.
11. Straighten your body and slip reins as you take off.
12. Use your seat bones and back muscles to push your horse on.
13. Learn how to fall!
14. Forget about the whip until you have gained a great deal of experience in keeping a horse well balanced

CHAPTER NINE

Hunting and 'Chasing

Dear Tom,

Overseas

First of all, my heartiest congratulations on winning three point-to-point races out of four starts, especially as the time of your third win was two seconds faster than the Open. But what bad luck you had at Buckfastleigh; I was very sad to read about Gosford Lass being badly kicked behind her knee, fracturing her excessary carpel bone before the start of her fifth race and that you had to withdraw her from the race. How disappointing for you! But that's the luck of racing, I am afraid. As your vet says, this means the end of her racing career. I think you are wise to compensate for your loss by having Gosford Lass covered this summer by a good stallion and I hope you breed your National winner! If you achieve your very ambitious aim of being the first owner-trainer-rider to win the great race, Gosford Lass's injury would certainly be a blessing in disguise.

The last time I wrote to you about hunting (see Chapter 3), I told you I would let you know what I tell any 'antis' who confront me with their ill-informed abuse. Our answer to their challenge is irrefutable, so don't hesitate to take up the challenge at any time of the day or night. Remember if you convert an 'anti', he or she in turn will probably convert several more. Don't reply to the accusation that foxhunting is cruel by saying the fox enjoys it, or that he needs the exercise because he doesn't, nor base your defence on economic grounds. That line will get you nowhere.

67

It is not the economics of the sport but its morality with which we are concerned. If your antagonist bases his attack on a question such as: 'Would you like to be chased by a pride of lions across country and then caught and eaten?' Your simple answer is that you would loathe it, but you are *not* a fox, you don't live in a hole, eat rats, mice, beetles and raw frogs, not to mention raw chicken. You do not kill every day just for the hell of it. But the fox does; his every meal is the product of a hunt and a kill. It is true we eat dead animals but so probably does your antagonist, and anyway unlike the fox you do not yourself slaughter them before filling your belly.

It just isn't possible to begin to compare the mental reactions of a human being and a fox. Every man and every animal alike fear death, but most humans and certainly all animals do not fear it until it is imminent. The fox must fear death, but only when he knows he is caught. The bullock does not tremble with fear on the way to the slaughter house because he doesn't know he is going to die, and likewise the fox doesn't tremble throughout the chase – in fact foxes have been known on numerous occasions to have stopped in the middle of a hunt to kill a chicken or duck! There can be no justifiable case for stating that the fox goes through an agonizing mental hell from the beginning until the end of the chase. On the contrary, all the evidence from a careful study of different foxes' behaviour during the chase indicates that he is not much worried until he knows he is cornered. Unlike a human being, the fox is himself a professional hunter and gets his living by stealth, and it is pointless equating his mental reaction to that of a human.

Another 'anti' war cry is that the odds are overwhelmingly against the fox. This is simply not borne out by the facts – only one in six foxes chased is killed. The fox sets the pace and only he knows the course which will be the one he considers most favourable to him. The fox is not chased until he drops from sheer exhaustion – he is chased until the superior speed and stamina of hounds enable them to overtake him. Remember the fox is very fit. He hunts every night for his food.

Finally, it is nonsense to say he is torn alive, limb by limb. The truth is he has very sharp teeth and he knows how to use them. Consequently, the leading hound knows that the only way to avoid a sharp bite is to catch the fox across the back and crunch. Instantly there is a broken back and numbness. One more crunch and the fox is dead.

To get rid of a known poultry thief, digging is sometimes necessary when a fox has gone to ground. Digging is cruel, but not nearly so cruel when done by the foxhunter as it would be if done by the local inhabitants. But this cruelty is fully recognised by the Foxhunting Powers That Be and they have ruled that the fox must be dug right out and despatched by a humane killer which every recognised hunt is required to carry.

Tom, if foxhunting were to cease, farmers would take the law into their own hands using any of the following methods:

(1) By trap. This is indeed a slow lingering death from starvation, during which time the fox is captive with all the fears and terrors of captive pain-wracked wild animals.

(2) By shotgun. If this method killed outright like an army rifle hitting a bull's eye, this would be a painless ending, but usually this is not the case – a shotgun fired in the dusk at extreme range is unlikely to kill dead but far more likely to wound, and as you probably know, a rat and fox do not lick their wounds; consequently a flesh wound may often prove fatal by gangrene. Ask an 'anti' if he thinks a pellet wound in the stomach, and a lingering death through gangrene is, to a fox, preferable to be hunted? Of course, it is *not*.

(3) By poison (which in any case is against the law). Ask

any 'anti' if he or she has ever seen the face of a dog or cat which had died of poison given by a human being. No 'anti' has probably seen this, but tell them to do so before they voice their foolish views again.

I am afraid I have wandered on about the morality of foxhunting, but it is a matter which we cannot afford to overlook – after all steeplechasing is called National *Hunt* racing, a fact which city punters often overlook.

From,

T.P.

SUMMARY

1. Luck plays a big part in racing.
2. The case for foxhunting against the 'antis'.
3. The alternatives are all more cruel and involve a slow painful death:
   (a) by trapping;
   (b) by shotgun wounds;
   (c) by poison (illegal).

PART TWO

A Pipe-Dream for Aintree

CHAPTER TEN

Breeding—and Point-to-Points

Dear Tom, Overseas

I am delighted to hear that you are determined to turn the ghastly kick Gosford Lass received into a glorious victory by breeding a Grand National winner! Nothing venture nothing gain, though I admit you are aiming at a very ambitious target, and you will have to dedicate all you've got to achieving it. It is no good hurrying such a plan and I think you ought to aim at the National in nine years time when your horse (i.e. Gosford Lass's first foal) is eight years old.

I suggest you plan on the following outline timetable:

1. *3-Year-Old*
   - (a) Spring   Lead in hand
     Lungeing
     Long Reining
     Loose Schooling
   - (b) June   Backing
     Elementary Riding Aids
     Initial Mounted Schooling
   - (c) Late Summer   At grass, supplemented by daily ration of oats
   - (d) Autumn   Hound Exercise
     Cub-hunting

2. *3–4 Year-Old* – Winter
   Oct-Feb   Regular Exercise
   Mounted Schooling

3. *4-Year-old*
   (a) March   Light hunting well within himself
   (b) April-June   At grass
   (c) July-Aug   Working hunter classes
   (d) Autumn   Cub-hunting

4. *4–5-Year-Old* – Winter
   Oct-Dec   Light hunting

5. *5-Year-Old*
   (a) Jan-Feb   Light hunting
   (b) March-April   Quiet hunting
                      Mounted schooling
   (c) April-June   At grass by night, in by day with a
                      ration of oats
   (d) July-Aug   Novice Show Jumping
   (e) Sept   Novice Hunter Trials
                      Novice One-Day Events
   (f) Oct-Dec   Regular Hunting

6. *6-Year-Old*
   (a) Jan-Feb   Fast schooling 'upsides'
   (b) March-May   Point-to-Points
   (c) May-June   At grass, supplemented by daily
                      ration of oats
   (d) Aug-Oct   Novice steeplechases
   (e) Oct-Dec   Regular Hunting

7. *7-Year-Old*
   (a) March-May   Hunterchases
   (b) May-June   At grass supplemented by daily
                      ration of oats
   (c) July   In by day, out at grass by night and
                      a daily ration of oats
   (d) Oct-Dec   3 mile Handicap Chases

8. *8-Year-Old*
   (a) Jan-March   3 mile Handicap Chases
   (b) End March   Grand National

You may be surprised to see I have included show jumping, hunter trials and even one-day events. This I have done advisedly because I do not think nowadays, due to wire, motorways, etc., that you get enough jumping experience out hunting and I am suggesting you remedy this deficiency by putting him in for show and cross country jumping competitions. I have been told that the 1965 National winner, Jay Trump, did some eventing in America so Gosford Lass's foal will be following good company!

Your first problem is the selection of a sire. I have had no practical experience of breeding, except pure bred Shetland ponies, and this letter is not written from experience, but deals with the theory. But I do know that there is no royal road to success in breeding steeplechasers.

However, before you start breeding long distance 'chasers, you must fully understand that breeding for steeplechasing is an expensive pastime. Profits are not large and results slow: it is a long time before horses are old enough or mature enough to run in, let alone win, steeplechases. Although horses have been known to win hunterchases at five years, they seldom reach their peak before seven or eight and this is a long period to keep a horse eating his head off with no return coming in.

It is important that youngsters are done well from the time they are born, but the most important time is the eleven months immediately prior to their birth and you *must*, and I repeat must, make certain that Gosford Lass is given the best of everything from the time of being covered until she drops her foal. As Harry Dufosee, who concentrates on breeding for steeplechasing and whose stock have won 119 N.H. races, told me when I last saw him at Wincanton, it is the early years in a horse's life which are of prime importance.

There is no doubt that stamina is a hereditary factor but whether it is passed on or not to a dam's progeny depends on a variety of things. First it depends on the heart and lung space, the length of limbs, constitution of muscles, tendons and ligaments and of course the temperament which will enable a placid horse not to take too much out of himself either before the race or in its early stages.

As I said earlier on, your first problem is to choose a stallion; don't ignore your local Hunter Improvement Stallion – if, like Spiritus did in the West Country, your local H.I.S. stallion is getting a number of point-to-point and hunterchase winners, it will save you a lot of money and give you a good chance of winning races, if you have your mare covered by him. It is, of course, difficult to select sires for steeplechasers because a 'chaser doesn't reach its prime before it is six or seven at the earliest, and consequently it is a lengthy business deciding whether a sire

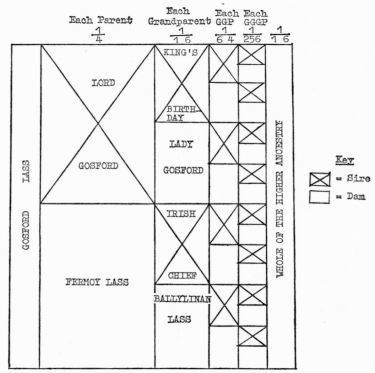

FIG. 1   Diagram showing Galton's Rule of Ancestral Contribution

is going to be a good jumping sire, and by the time his progeny have proved him, he may well be past his best, if not already dead. I don't believe it is necessary for a jumper to be 'jumping-bred' on both sides of his pedigree. I personally am a great believer in Galtons' Rule of Ancestral Contribution. This rule considers that $\frac{1}{4}$ of each parents' characteristics, in particular their performance, soundness and temperament, are passed on. 1/16 of each grandparents' characteristics, 1/64 of each great grand-parents', 1/256 of each great great grandparents' and 1/16 of the whole of the earlier ancestry. This is diagrammatic-ally illustrated by Gosford Lass's pedigree (Fig. 1). Of course some people are strongly in favour of Bruce Lowe's theories and will tell you that Galtons' Rule is wrong. But if you agree with Galtons' Theory, the sire may pass on his speed and Gosford Lass her jumping ability. However, as I have already intimated, growth is dependent mainly on nourishment, both during the eleven months in the dam's womb and in its early years, the most important period being the pre-natal eleven months. It is however a fact that progeny by a small stallion out of a big mare will be larger in size than one by a big stallion out of a small mare, which is fortunate because Gosford Lass must be at least 16 ft 1 in if not 16 ft 2 in.

The next thing you must consider is the time to cover Gosford Lass. For flat racing, because the advantages of an early foal two years later are marked, it is necessary to cover the mare in February, but unlike flat racing a foal, destined to make his mark point-to-pointing and hunter-chasing, will not be required to exert itself until it is four years old, by which time it will make little difference whether it was foaled in January or May. In fact I would go as far as saying that April/May is the better time to foal because the spring grass is at its sweetest in late April and May. If therefore you intend having Gosford Lass's first foal in May next year, she must have her covered early in June this year, which will just give you time to rough her off now and give her the eight clear weeks she needs to allow her muscles to be sufficiently relaxed for her first service.

From,

T.P.

P.S.

You mentioned in your last letter that you might take over the duties of the Point-to-Point Secretary, I think this an excellent idea and I can write on this subject with recent practical experience. I always find it helpful to make out an annual timetable so that I didn't overlook anything. I am pinning to this letter a suggested timetable with two annexes attached and a final checklist of the point-to-point secretary's duties. Of course different hunts may have slightly different duties but in the main they are the same. You will see there is quite a lot to be done, so don't take it on unless you think you have the time to do it properly. I don't think many owners and riders often realise how much work goes into organising a point-to-point meeting!

POINT-TO-POINT

Approximate Outline Annual Timetable

August: Read Weatherbys' *Regulations and Explanatory Notes* booklet.

September: Try to get sponsors for each race. Get advertisers for programmes. Call Committee Meeting to decide conditions of Races, etc. Attend Area Meeting to decide dates of 1971 Meetings. Bid for the second Saturday in April. After the meeting send Area Chairman a list of entries with owners' addresses from previous season's records. As soon as date has been agreed at both meetings send to Weatherbys' £20 plus application form for meeting (see 'Explanatory Notes' *Jockey Club Booklet*, Page 2 & 3 – Para 1.1 & format).

October: Receive from Weatherbys' approval of dates of Meeting. Receive a copy of *Annual Point-to-Point Regulations*. Read them to see if there are any new rules since previous year. Send Area Chairman conditions of next seasons races at our Point-to-Point.

November: Receive consolidated list of owners from Area Chairman (address of owners who entered for previous season (point-to-point) meetings).

December: Contact printers about a poster for next year.

January: Call Committee Meeting to decide officials, confirm race conditions, etc., arrange for rebuilding of jumps, etc. Invite officials (See Annex A page 82) to officiate. Order badges from Nicholsons (See Annex B page 83). Order car stickers from printers. Receive booklet of area point-to-point schedules.

February: If advertising space still available in programme, try to fill it.

March: Distribute posters – Hunt Supporters' Club will help. Invite Course Inspector to view course (at least one jump) four weeks before meeting (*Jockey Club Booklet* Page 9 Para 4.3). Keep a reserve of entry forms for people who write and ask for race conditions. Distribute car stickers – Hunt Supporters' Club will help. Arrange advertising in local papers. Send all other Hunt Secretaries a complimentary car pass. It has also been customary to send past point-to-point secretaries of the hunt concerned a complimentary car pass each.

Make arrangements for the following:

Police (write to Chief Inspector in area).
St John Ambulance (men plus an ambulance).
Weighing Machine from local coal merchants.
Hire of tents. Toilets.
Hire of broadcasting and commentary equipment.
Valet to be present in men's changing tent.
Caterers.
Sufficient number cloths.
Insurance with local insurance brokers.
Jump Stewards and their flags.
Flags for Mounted Stewards.
Flags for weigh-in, objection, objection over-ruled, objection upheld.

April: Confirm all arrangements have been made in accordance with the regulations.

Write to 1970 winners telling them to return cups at the meeting. As soon as entries close send Weatherbys' a list of entries on their special form.

On the Monday you will receive a list of all horses qualified to run in point-to-point. If any entry does not come in this list, the owner must be told that he cannot run (see *Jockey Club Booklet* Page 6, Para. 3.1 & 3.2).

Finance: Keep a record of all your expenditure. The Point-to-Point account is held at the local bank. The bank sends out at your request two cashiers to deal with the cash coming in from the sale of car passes and programmes and also small change which is required by car pass and programme sellers.

Customs and Excise: You also have to inform the Customs and Excise people of the meeting.

Tote: Send a complimentary car pass for their bus, also put their notices up.

Bookmakers: They will bring you money to pay into the cashiers, plus a form to send to Manchester. The local representative of the Customs and Excise will explain the regulations to you.

After the meeting send a marked card to Weatherbys' and the format on Page 23 of the instructional *Jockey Club Booklet. Get two Stewards to sign it at the meeting to save sending it around for signature.*

ANNEX A

OFFICIALS TO BE INVITED BY THE SECRETARY ON BEHALF OF THE POINT-TO-POINT COMMITTEE

TO BE INCLUDED ON PROGRAMME	Stewards (Joint Masters invite these) Judge (Invited by Joint Masters) Starter Assistant Starter Clerk of the Scales Hon. Med. Officers Hon. Vet. Hon. Farriers Clerk of Course Hon. Sec.
ALSO	Announcer Commentator Valet Official in charge of car park arrangements Official in charge of sale of programmes Mounted Stewards Clerk to whom declarations are made Official in charge of number board Official in charge of number cloths

82

BADGES AND PRINTING TO BE DONE

Nicholsons
1×Declaration Book – 5 races
1×Declaration Pad
1 set Judge's Result Cards
150 Declarations Forms
400 Shield Shape Hunt Enclosure Badges
5 sets Grooms' Arm Badges Nos. 1–24 (depending on number of entries)
Officials' Badges Style 'A'

Printers
300 Car Stickers
2500–3000 Race Cards
8 Books of 50 x £2.50 Car Passes
12 Books of 50 x £1.50 Car Passes
2 Books of 50 x Complimentary Passes

FINAL CHECKLIST

Arrangements must be made for:
1. Police.
2. St John Ambulance (or other first aid helpers, i.e. Red Cross).
3. Stewards (invited by Masters).
4. Badges from Nicholson's of Gillingham, Dorset.
5. Number cloths.
6. Informing Local Rep of the Custom and Excise.
   (a) Bookmakers provide betting duty sheet on the day which must be sent to Manchester).
7. Tote (Notices must be posted at each end. Sent by Totalisator Board).
8. Insurance:
   (a) for Abandonment ⎫
   (b) Committee Accident ⎬ through Local Insurance Brokers.
   (c) Third Party ⎭
9. Tents (hire of and erection).
10. Weighing Machine – borrowed from local coal merchants.
11. Hon. Medical Officers, Vets, etc., as stated on the programme.
12. Two Union Jacks for finishing post.
13. Two White flags for starter and his assistant.
14. Mounted Stewards
15. All other stores (e.g. car park notices, Jump Steward discs, Jump Steward flags).
16. Flags required for Mounted Stewards.
17. Coloured flags (blue for weighed in, red for objection).
18. Weatherbys:
    (a) apply for Meeting and send £20.
    (b) after meeting, send marked programme.
    (*Note* Read *Weatherbys' Regulations* and explanatory notes for current year).
19. Attend Area Point-to-Point Meeting and bid for date (e.g. 2nd Saturday in April).

20. Send list of addresses or previous year's entries to Chairman of Area Meeting.
21. Advertising – Contact local printers about posters.
22. Programmes – Send list of entries to Weatherbys' and receive a list of qualified horses (see *Regulations*).
23. Send past secretaries complimentary tickets.
24. Course Inspector – see regulations.
25. Gratuities Police – Valet (Mr Steer).
26. Caterers.
27. Cashiers from bank.
28. Send other point-to-point secretaries in area complimentary tickets.

SUMMARY

1. An ideal eight year preparation programme for the Grand National!
2. Breeding for steeplechasing is an expensive and slow pastime.
3. The eleven months before birth are the most important.
4. Give the young horse the best of everything, but give it in moderation and wisely.
5. Don't disregard your local H.I.S. Stallion.
6. Galtons' Rule of Ancestral Contribution.
7. Early foal for flat racing, but spring foal for steeplechasing.
8. A point-to-point secretary is a very busy man!

CHAPTER ELEVEN

Making the Young Horse (3 years old)

Dear Tom,

In my last letter I wrote to you about breeding; in this letter I propose giving you some guide lines on 'making' her first foal. By 'making' I mean breaking, backing, teaching the elementary riding aids and starting his jumping education. I do not think that any oats are necessary for a young unbroken thoroughbred as they tend to go to his head, like strong drink to a young man, but by all means give him as much hay as he requires and add some grass if possible. Jack Barratt used to tell me when I had horses in training with him that, in his opinion, the making of an unbroken youngster destined for the steeplechase course (or indeed for the hunter) was the most important time in the horse's career.

The first phase should be as long a period as possible and consist of getting him used to the feel of human hands on his body, and more particularly on his head. Rub his belly and pull his ears, in fact do anything which will accustom him to human touch. Also train him at an early stage to pick his feet up, and also at this stage get him used to dogs of all kinds. In this phase I strongly recommend that all horses should begin their jumping education by jumping him riderless either in a school or alternatively in a jumping lane with the jump merely a log or pole lying on the ground. This is his first lesson in jumping.

86

Begin leading him out in hand in the spring when he is three years old. After about a week of leading him out it should be possible to progress to the second phase which is lungeing. During his lungeing lesson try to get him to recognise and obey the spoken words of command such as 'whoa', 'prepare to trot' and 'trot'. Start by restricting his lungeing lessons to about thirty minutes and don't forget to lunge him both clockwise and anti-clockwise. Every time he obeys an order correctly, give him some oats or sugar so that he connects obedience with reward. To prevent boredom when lungeing, you, as the trainer, should walk slowly in a big circle around the field so that the horse instead of making circle, makes an oval circuit.

It is a good thing when lungeing your horse in a field to arrange for him to pass close to a variety of country sights, such as farm animals, including pigs of which he will almost certainly show signs of fear at first sight. But patience will work wonders and it is surprising how a patient trainer can, by persevering, overcome the horses natural fear of any unusual object. After about seven days of lungeing the youngster around a field, you can continue his jumping instruction very unambitiously by merely lungeing him over a pole lying on the ground in the path of his lungeing oval circuit; when he disregards the pole, raise it about six inches. The lungeing phase need not take more than two or three weeks.

After the lungeing phase, the third phase of his training is the 'bitting' phase. The object of the 'bitting' phase is to get the horse accustomed to having something, which will later be used to control him, through the very *sensitive* mouth, with which all horses are born. Quite simply it merely involves putting a snaffle in his mouth with the reins knotted over his neck, but you must be very careful not to fall into three traps. These are; firstly, making the young horse's mouth sore so that he won't go up to his bit; secondly, making him overbent and, thirdly, giving him a dead mouth. I have often been told that it is a good idea to get the horse used to the bit in his box, by allowing him to stand for half an hour at a time with the bit in his mouth but no pressure on it. Continue this for about a fortnight and you then come to the next obstacle which is putting the roller on. Getting this on and fastened under his belly is likely to worry the young horse and I suggest that, having successfully got it on, you leave him in his box for twenty-four to forty-eight hours to get used to it. This is the introduction to the fourth phase (i.e. long reining) because until you have achieved getting the roller on, it is impossible to long rein him.

Long reining is the method used to obtain more control over, and instil more discipline into the horse than can be done with the lungeing rein, and secondly of course, to 'mouth' him by which I mean accustom him to being controlled by long reins using the bit. As you haven't had any experience in long reining, I suggest you begin by practising on an old horse. It is not an easy art and even with an aged animal you will make plenty of mistakes. Then when you have gained experience and confidence on an older horse, I suggest you do not attempt to combine the two objectives of long reining, but achieve them in two stages. If I were you I would limit the first stage to long reining him using the head collar 'Ds' for steering together with use of your voice and then go on to the second stage in which you can attach the long reins to the bit and thus get him accustomed to being controlled by the mouth. It is important to get the horse to relax the lower jaw from the earliest phases of his training – this can be achieved by getting the horse to play with whatever is in his mouth and I advise you to secure an end of a curb chain by string to one of the snaffle rings and pass the chain through the horse's mouth with the links uneven (i.e. not smooth as when fitted to a curb bit). Fix the other end of the chain to the opposite snaffle ring so that the chain hangs loosely in the mouth but below the bit and is not stretched too taut across the mouth but don't let him get his tongue over it. You do, I suppose, realise that if the lower jaw is relaxed it is a physical impossibility for any horse to pull. As Tony Collins used to tell me when he was training me at Porlock for the 1951 three-day event at Badminton, 'Get your horse to chew on his bit'. And another thing I must stress is that you must make maximum use of your voice, an invaluable aid during the whole of the lungeing and long reining phases. Great care must be taken with both the long reins and, later, when ridden that there is an equal pressure on both sides of his mouth so that he does not become one-sided. If your young animal contracts any bad habits such as getting his tongue over the bit, it is *essential* to prevent them taking root as it is very very difficult to cure a horse of his fault later on, and a most infuriating and irritating thing to happen as it virtually takes the horse out of your (the rider's) control. Tom, if your horse shows signs of doing this, check that the bit isn't too low in his mouth; if it is raise it as high as you can without unduly wrinkling the corners of his lips. If this does not work, try another bit, particularly if the one you are using is a jointed snaffle as this type of bit by its very nature sags down in the horse's mouth and thus encourages him to get his tongue back and over it. If you are faced with this problem, I suggest you try him in a straight bar half-moon vulcanite snaffle.

The fifth phase in making the young horse is backing him. First of all, get him used to the saddle without leathers. Let him stand in his box or in the stable yard for some hours before you take him out with the saddle on. When he is absolutely quiet and happy with the saddle on, put on some additional weight using a weight cloth and lead, working up from seven pounds to about four stone, adding half a stone each day for eight days. Then, when he is quite used to carrying weight on his back, very carefully by slow stages put a foot in one iron, then put some weight on the iron, then be given a leg up and lie across the horse's saddle on your stomach, making a fuss of the horse on its off-side, and finally mount and sit astride him; during these four latter mounting stages make quite certain that someone, whom the young horse knows and in whom he has confidence, is standing by his head talking to him all the time, and holding his head gently but firmly by the reins. Next, progress from sitting astride to being led round the yard, then round the field in which he has been lunged and finally, being ridden out at a walk without escort. Fortunately, Tom, you have good hands because it is abolutely imperative that the rider has good hands and that he rides with fairly long stirrup leathers.

During the long rein training the horse has been impelled forward as a result of the use of the voice and light lungeing whip. Little or no pressure has been used on the mouth. But once you have reached the mounted part of your training, you must teach your horse to allow a certain amount of bearing to be taken on the bars of his mouth, and to go forward as a result of the impulsion received from your lower legs and seat bones. In the very early stages when you draw your lower leg slightly to the rear and squeeze just behind the girth your horse will not understand the signal or aid, and therefore you should carry *two* long polo whips and simultaneously with your leg pressure, gently flick both whips (one in each hand) behind the legs, and he will go forward associating the forward impulsion with the leg pressure behind the girth. When you have built up complete mutual confidence at a walk, you can try him at a trot. The whole period of backing from when you first sit astride him at the halt until you are trotting him unescorted should not take more than a week. Start this fifth stage with no oats, but gradually after about ten days give him some oats very gradually increasing the quantity as you would with an older horse just up from grass, but over the following five or six weeks, when he is doing riding school work, do not exceed five to seven pounds per day.

The sixth and final phase in 'making' the young horse is normal school work. During this phase your aim to teach him the aids before asking him to obey them. If he is 'put to the aids' correctly he will have a good basis on which to build for whatever future equestrian activity he is destined. By 'putting to the aids' I mean training him to be fully relaxed, to have no tension nor rigidity of any kind in either his jaws, his poll, his neck, his back or, in fact, anywhere. This school work consists of standing, walking, trotting, halting, circling, cantering and finally, if you wish to, you can introduce him to the double bridle during this phase but as he is destined for the racecourse, I do not think you need bother. You will find later that the more your horse responds to the aids during this elementary dressage school work the more willingly will he be to stand back and soar over his fences. But don't think that it is easy to ride a completely green horse because it most definitely is not, even to the most experienced riders. You will find that the horse never feels completely under control and gives the impression of his quarters and hindlegs not being co-ordinated with his shoulders and forelegs. But although I know it is difficult, green horse can be taught the aids as soon as he has been backed, walked and trotted out freely. A whip is needed to make the horse understand the meaning of the rider's urging with the lower leg and seat bones, but be very careful not to frighten or startle him by using the whip without due caution.

Once the horse associates the squeezing of the lower legs with a forward movement, all further work can be done at a quiet trot – just a trifle faster than the horse goes voluntarily. As soon as the horse slackens or shortens his stride is the time to urge him on with the lower legs and seat bones, and it is then that the rider starts imposing his will on the horse.

Changes of pace must all be done stage by stage. One small success will follow after another and often after a short time the horse will understand what is required of him when the rider's legs squeeze is increased. But it is of vital importance that the riders hands do not exert any pressure on the horses mouth via the reins, the horse must be given no excuse for letting his head come behind the vertical line. Remember the horse must never be behind the bit, and this can only be stopped by increased urging with the legs and seat, and only if this fails should you resort to tapping with the whip and even then, only a very light tap. The best indication of success in training your mount can be seen by the firmness and steadiness of the forward stride. By your supple and quiet seat, you should be able to gradually increase your back action (which is much the same as when propelling a swing forward) during the halts, and your young mount can be said to 'be at the aids'.

Your increased back action, coupled with increased lower leg pressure and a firm seat will bring your horse automatically up into his bridle.

Concurrently with all six phases continue his dismounted jumping lessons, first loose and then on the lungeing rein but very *gradually* raising the jumping pole from the ground to two feet, but when you have reached one and a half feet add small wings to the jump, thus removing any temptation to run out. After he has jumped two feet on the lungeing rein erect a 'lane' consisting of two parallel sides about sixty yards long and place poles in the lane at varying distances apart including some very close together so that he learns to be clever and find the proverbial fifth leg. But don't overface him at this stage and I should be content with poles at a height of between ground level and one and a half feet, and not less than nine feet apart. First of all jump him loose down the lane, and then jump him mounted over the same small obstacles; but never at this stage, however fluently he jumps, raise the poles higher than two feet.

These six phases in making a young horse should have taken from the spring when he was three years old until the end of June, although of course the earlier you start letting him get used to your hands on his body (Phase 1), the better. Then turn him out by night and in by day until the autumn when he can be exercised with hounds, and later cub-hunted well within himself with a competent light-weight rider with good hands.

During the winter when he is three to four years old, give him regular exercise and more schooling and in the following spring hunt him lightly at the end of the season.

From,

T.P.

SUMMARY

1. Making includes breaking, backing, teaching the elementary riding aids and starting a horse's jumping education.
2. Oats are not necessary for a young unbroken thoroughbred.
3. Six phases of making the young horse:
   (a) Fondling the youngster's head and body with human hands
   (b) Lungeing
   (c) Bitting
   (d) Long reining
   (e) Backing   } +The Jumping Lane
   (f) Normal school work

CHAPTER TWELVE

Schooling, Dressage and Eventing

Overseas

Dear Tom,

We will assume that you have accepted the outline time-table (see page 74) as suggested in an earlier letter on breeding, and that the colt, which you have had gelded (we will call him for convenience Gosford Lad) is now five years old and having been successfully shown in working hunter classes as a four-year-old and after a season light hunting, is now out at grass. Bring him in from grass at the end of June and prepare him to increase his jumping experience, for a few novice show jumping competitions at the smaller local shows towards the end of July and in August. As I explained to you when I proposed the outline eight year programme to you, I do not think you get enough jumping nowadays out hunting, certainly in the West Country, and Gosford Lad needs all the jumping experience you can give him to make him clever. You will remember that was why the show jumping, hunter trials and one-day events were included in his programme (see plate 9 page 65). In the old days I think a season's hunting would have given him all the jumping required, this will be more than remedied by schooling and preparing him for a couple of day events at Cullompton and Powderham Castle.

Most people regard dressage as more of a mystery than any other aspect of riding. This is quite wrong. It is true that it requires in its more advanced tests a very high standard of horsemanship indeed. But in the B.H.S. Dressage Test No. 2 which is used in Novice Horse Trials such as the two I have mentioned, all that is required is a horse which has trained to be supple, well balanced, collected and obedient to the elementary aids given by the rider. The conditions of the Test No. 2 lay down that the horse is to be ridden in a snaffle. To get him supple the best exercise to teach him is the shoulder-in. This exercise is a development of the circle. For example, assume you are riding Gosford Lad in a rectangular riding school at a sitting trot around a left handed circle. This in itself, if the circle is small, is not an easy exercise for the horse because his off fore and off hind are travelling a greater distance than his near ones. This would not matter much if it didn't mean that the near hindleg has to make a shorter stride simultaneously with the off foreleg making a bigger stride, the smaller the circle the bigger the difference in length of strides, and it is of course the opposite when the off hindleg moves simultaneously with the near foreleg. This accounts for the difficulty you have in keeping the horse's rhythm unchanged when riding in *small* circles at a sitting trot. It is not an easy exercise for the horse and it takes time to get correct. On the left handed circle the inside legs carry more of the horse and rider's weight than to the off (outer) legs. This especially affects the near hindleg which has to develop much greater energy. Now once you have got Gosford Lad trotting (sitting) in rhythm in a circle select a convenient point where the circle meets the side of the rectangular school, be it an indoor one or outdoor. (An indoor one is easier as there will not be so much to see to distract Gosford Lad's attention.) When Gosford Lad's quarters arrive at the selected point, you as the rider are required to 'push' him sideways along a tangent to his circle, moving on two tracks by which I mean a movement on which the horse's hind feet follow a different one to his fore feet. He should still be bent and flexed as he was on the circle and when done well the horse's body should be at an angle of about 30 degrees with the line of his advance down the side of the school.

In this left shoulder-in exercise, the near hindleg has to work much harder than the off one because it has to move sideways underneath the body to take the weight of the horse and rider. If Gosford Lad loses either impulsion or rhythm, all you need do is to resume the circle (see circle B in diagram below) until he has regained his impulsion and rhythm. Of course, start with a large circle which will require less flexion and make it easier for the horse; go from the circle to the left shoulder-in exercise by pushing the horses body along the new line of advance with your left leg, simultaneously carrying both hands and reins towards the right, the left rein assisting to push the quarters to the right by acting as rein of opposition to the haunches. The shoulder-in exercise is essentially a schooling one and not required in dressage tests.

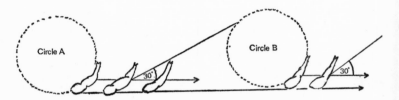

FIG. 2   The left shoulder-in exercise

This shoulder-in exercise may sound rather complicated but the diagram above illustrates it when viewed from above and make it quite easy to understand. When you first start to teach Gosford Lad this exercise, I stress make a large circle and, as he becomes more supple, you can reduce the radius.

To get him well 'bent' inward when circling, have your inner leg vertical down the girth and bend his forehand inward by tightening the inner rein at the same time as you loosen the outer rein, and bend his hindquarters inward by carrying your outside leg back slightly behind the girth and pushing his hindquarters inward, thus you are bending him inwards around your own vertical inner leg.

Both the horse and rider must be well balanced. You can test your balance by quitting the irons, and crossing the leathers over in front of the saddle. In the early stages of making him as a three-year-old, as soon as he was backed, you will remember you taught him the elementary aids. To do the dressage test well, Gosford Lad must be completely relaxed, and understand the influence of the rider's legs, hands, weight and back muscles. He must show quiet, regular but lively steps. He should carry his head at the same height and move forward perfectly straight; when cornering or turning he must be able to flex towards the inside – if he glances, even the smallest possible amount, outwards, he will convey the impression of stiffness. He should never get his tongue over the bit nor let it hang out of the side of his mouth. He must never shake his head, even when halting or changing gait. His neck should be nicely rounded and finally he must carry his tail quietly without swishing it. If you have achieved all these requirements you can congratulate yourself on having got Gosford Lad supple and relaxed. You are teaching him collection all the time in your schoolwork, including every single half halt, but beware when you are trying to increase the bend of the poll and neck that you do not fall into the trap of trying to obtain it by pulling on the reins, as this will only result in either the horse 'leaning' on the bit or worse still, getting behind the bit.

For the one-day event dressage test, the rider must be able to sit steadily at the lowest part of the saddle with his arms and hands completely quiet. The reins must be continuously taut and contact with the horse's mouth must *never* be obtained by jerking the reins. Finally the rider's legs must be quietly and continuously in contact with the horse's body so that they can act instantaneously without it being necessary to alter their position. The only movement made is the very slight bending of the knee to squeeze him forward, like squeezing a tube of toothpaste as Colonel

Hance put it when he was teaching me before the 1951 Badminton Three-Day Event.

This training in dressage will not only teach him balance and collection, but also assist his rider start him off on the correct leg at the start of a race. Such much for dressage.

After his show jumping and eventing experience he will then of course have to be taught to jump at racing speed before he appears on a racecourse, but I will cover this in my next letter.

From,

T.P.

SUMMARY

1. A vast amount of jumping all types of obstacles is needed to make a horse a good and clever jumper.
2. Nowadays because in most hunting countries the amount of jumping is limited by motorways and wire, hunter trials and one-day events provide the extra jumping experience required to develop 'fifth leg'.
3. Dressage is not a mystery.
4. For Novice Horse Trials, a horse must be supple, well balanced, collected and obedient to the elementary aids.
5. The Shoulder-In exercise.

CHAPTER THIRTEEN

Schooling for Steeplechasing

Dear Tom,

I was delighted to hear how well Gosford Lad performed at Powderham One-Day Event, and that you have decided to let him down to give him a short rest in October before you hunt him regularly to qualify him in November and December and then get him ready to start his race career in point-to-points next March. With all the jumping experience he has gained this past summer and autumn plus two season's hunting he should give you some great point-to-point rides next spring.

However, you will find that Gosford Lad will be jumping safely but rather too cautiously for racing after his show jumping, hunter trials and eventing and of course as the East Devon is mainly a banking country, most of Gosford Lad's jumping out hunting will have been done off his hocks from a collected trot or canter. For jumping at racing pace, the fences are cleared from a good gallop and it is the momentum given by his speed added to the spring from his hocks which carries him over and through the top inch or so of the fences. The requirement therefore is to put up two flights of hurdles in the paddock at Gosford and build two schooling fences facing the stables as he will be more enthusiastic if he is jumping towards home. Hurdles can be purchased quite easily, and all you need do is to pack them with gorse off Woodbury Common, or if this is not available, use birch or even privet. To make your schooling fences, dig a trench twelve inches deep, erecting a strong

99

rail on the landing side about one and three-quarter foot high against which you can lay your birch, which is much the best material for a schooling fence. By having the rail about one foot away on the landing side you can get the birch to slop nicely. When you have packed the birch really *tightly*, place the guard rail on the take-off side, and paint the top few inches of the guard rail a mat colour, such as steel grey. You can easily make your fence into an open ditch by placing a log about four feet from the trench on the take-off side. (Turn to the diagrams at the end of this letter for the dimensions of regulation point-to-point fences). There is no need to school over a water jump although I have done so in the past; I remember I schooled a Devon farmer's maiden point-to-point horse over schooling fences with corrugated iron sheets on the landing side to represent water. However, Michael Scudamore once said to me: 'The water jump never need bother anyone provided they ride hard at it because the horse's momentum will carry him over the water'. This I am sure is quite correct, particularly with the new Jockey Club water jump; It is not often appreciated that a horse can easily clear a spread of about sixteen feet from a trot out hunting so you will readily appreciate the wisdom of Michael Scudamore's remark.

Always wear a regulation helmet when schooling even over hurdles. I made the mistake of not wearing one when schooling for Jack Barratt on a Saturday and woke up on Sunday morning in Salisbury hospital with concussion and a cracked vertebra in my spine.

Fortunately you have good hands and are pretty strong because these two, together with determination are the essential qualities for a good schooling jockey. Never let a young point-to-point horse run out or refuse when schooling him, so make sure that you have adequate wings to your schooling hurdles and fences, and always school an inexperienced 'chaser like Gosford Lad with an old campaigner. The latter can first of all give Gosford Lad a lead over the hurdles – about half a dozen lengths in front – and then as soon as Gosford Lad has gained confidence, probably after three or four times, the next progression in his schooling is to allow him to jump 'upsides' the older horse. You will find that this smartens him up a lot. Sooner or later Gosford Lad will almost certainly make a mistake, and both the rap and the banging nose of hurdle might well have shaken his confidence without the previous benefit of his experience in the hunting field and eventing. But as he is such a bold jumper, a mistake like this should do no harm at all, and may well have the desirable effect in the future of making him pay a little more respect to his hurdles and fences, which is not a bad thing for a potential Grand National candidate! When you are satisfied that he is jumping the hurdles fluently 'upsides', give him a lead over the fences, and again when you are satisfied let him jump these 'upsides' the older horse.

The all important factor is the take-off, and I think it will be obvious to you that the faster the pace the more difficult it will be to adjust the length of stride to ensure that he takes-off from the right position – the normal distance of take-off from the jump being about one and a half times the height of the jump (e.g. for a four foot jump a bold 'chaser should take-off about six feet in front of the take-off board). But the more you school your youngster to stand back and take-off outside the wings the better because it is in the air that he can gain a length at each jump. A horse normally judges his take-off position from the take-off board, and if you place a pole on the ground one or two feet in front of the take-off board, this will encourage him to stand back. If he takes off too soon his momentum will usually carry him over and through the top of the jump without any ill effects which is why most horses jump the open ditch better than any other jump. But if, on the other hand, Gosford Lad gets too close to his fences, he will not then have enough room to reach the top of his jumping parabola before reaching the fence with the result that he will hit the fence lower down, where it is thicker and stiffer, which will probably end in disaster. In the extreme cases where a horse takes-off very close to the fence it is called, as you no-doubt know, 'taking the fence by the roots'!

All horses have a tendency to take-off simultaneously, as I told you in my letter on race riding tactics (see Chapter 8), so try not to get half-lengthed when schooling 'upsides' because if the other horses stands well back, it is possible that Gosford Lad may take-off simultaneously and, having stood too far back, fail to clear the fence. But many more horses fall through taking-off too close to the jump then do through standing back too far.

It is also very important that 'chasers don't dwell on leading, so from the beginning of his schooling over hurdles and fences you must always 'pick him up' on landing and teach him to get away into his stride without delay.

By a combination of standing back at his fences and getting into his stride again immediately on landing, he can easily gain a length at each fence, and eighteen lengths so gained in a three mile chase represents about seventy yards; if Gosford Lad can gain a length at each fence in the Grand National he will have an advantage of about 100 yards, which is tremendous help!

I quite forgot to mention earlier that, as Gosford Lad has never been in race training before, you will probably have to teach him how to gallop. To do this I am told the best method is to use a standing martingale and adjust it so that he cannot raise his nose higher than his withers.

From,

T.P.

P.S.

I have pinned to this letter details on the construction of fences based on the specifications that we used when building the 1972 East Devon point-to-point jumps. I think you will find it useful when constructing your schooling fences. Your schooling fences should be just as thick as the point-to-point regulations ones, but can be an inch or two lower.

POINT-TO-POINT STEEPLECHASES

1. *Height of Fences*
Fences should not be less than four feet three inches, measured from the take-off side to the highest point (A–B) except in the case of a water jump or where the nature of the ground justified some variation.

2. *Plain Fences*
It is suggested that all plain fences should be built on a base of about five feet 6 inches (C–D) and the slope of the fence should reduce the thickness at the top to about twelve inches. (E–F). The base measurement is calculated as the distance from the take-off board, or apron to a point on the landing side vertically below the overhang of the birch.

3. *Open Ditches*
The width of this fence at the top is recommended as being about 2 feet (L–M) and the width of the ditch five feet measured from the front edge of the frame on the take-off side to the front of the guard rail (O–P).

4. *Frames*
It is suggested that no timber used in the construction of any frame should be higher than twenty-two inches from ground level. (J–K).

5. *Guard Rails*
(a) *For Open Ditch*

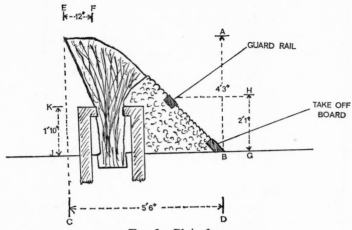

FIG. 3.   Plain fence

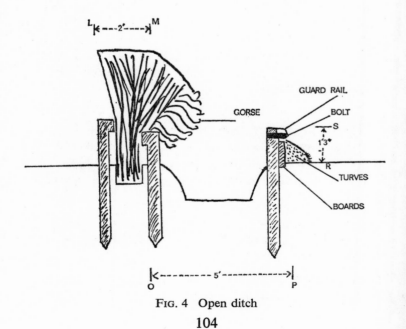

FIG. 4   Open ditch

The top few inches of the pole of the guard rail must be painted a light colour, e.g. Seville 1806, a Dulux paint and the rail recommended as being between twelve inches and eighteen inches high (R–S). The Boards beneath the rail (in cases where a turf facing is not used) should be either battleship grey or some other neutral colour, or creosoted. To prevent shine, a gloss finish must not be used.

(b) *For Plain Fence*

Where these are used they should be painted a light colour, e.g. Seville 1806 and a gloss finish must not be used. The top of the guard rail should not be higher than twenty-five inches (i.e. half the height of the fence) from ground level, and must be recessed into the line of the fence. (G–H).

6. *Take-off Boards*

Where provided, these must be painted a light colour, e.g. Seville 1806, a Dulux paint, but the paint again must not be shiny.

7. *Wings*

The recommended height where wings join a fence is about six feet and the length should be about eighteen inches.

SUMMARY

1. Having schooling jumps facing towards the stables.
2. Always school in company with another horse.
3. First school over hurdles, then over fences.
4. Jumping upsides smartens a horse up.
5. Encourage horses to stand well back.
6. Teach 'chasers not to dwell on landing.
7. A young horse may have to be taught how to gallop.
8. Construction of Point-to-Point fences.

CHAPTER FOURTEEN

'Chasing and Aintree

Overseas

Dear Tom,

I am delighted that your single-mindedness of purpose and racing luck (and skill!) held good for not only your point-to-point last year, but also for the novice 'chases in the last autumn and Gosford Lad's hunter chases this past spring.

I am particularly glad that you took full advantage of his 'Novice At Closing' engagements and gave him four novice 'chases in quick succession, before he became ineligible for Novice 'chases. I am a firm believer in wrapping horses up in cotton wool when in stables, but riding them like hell on the racecourse. As long as a horse is fit and well, and eats up his feed, I think there is no harm at all in racing horses often when they have reached their peak of fitness. I can see no reason at all against racing placid horses, which are all good doers, in five races a fortnight, or even in races on two consecutive days, and then giving them a rest, possibly including a day's hunting for a change. I can remember Waking running third in a three mile 'chase at Wincanton on Boxing Day 1955, and then turning out again on 27th December to run a hell of a good race at Taunton where he was again 'in the money'. I also gave Tullaherin Lord a very hard race in the Grand Military Gold Cup at Sandown Park in 1960 when he came a close up fourth, and then after liberal quantities of glucose, turning him out again on the second day of the Grand Military Meeting when he gave me a great ride to

106

come second to Pointsman and after all, Pointsman was really in a different class to the type of horse you normally expect to compete in the Grand Military Hunterchase!

It is also highly satisfactory to hear that you qualified him in one of his hunterchase engagements for the Grand National. You can now select his engagements in preparation for the National next season without having to worry about whether they will qualify him for the National or not.

Although I have just told you not to be afraid of running your horses frequently; as this coming season is going to be aimed specifically at preparing Gosford Lad for the Grand National, I don't think you should take any risks with him and I suggest you reduce his engagements to about half a dozen leading up to his peak of fitness at the end of March on Grand National Day. Gosford Lad has quite a lot in common with both Jay Trump and Freddie who were first and second respectively in the 1965 National. Jay Trump and Freddie were both eight-year-olds, they both had the National as their main goal, Jay Trump could put up a good performance in one-day events, and Freddie's racing career started in races confined to hunters, Jay Trump was ridden by an amateur in the great race, and Freddie trained by an amateur.

I think it, therefore, a good idea to have a look at the 1964–65 Chase-form, and see what preparatory engagements these two successful Aintree horses were given. They were:

	Joy Trump	*Freddie*
1st Race	21st Oct 3m Autumn Trial Chase Sandown Park	17th Oct 3m Joan Mackay Steeplechase Ayr
2nd Race	20th Nov 3m Handicap Chase Windsor	21st Nov 3m Stanley Tools Handicap Chase, Doncaster

A Pipe-Dream for Aintree

	Joy Trump	Freddie
3rd Race	26th Dec 3m K.G. VI Chase Kempton Park	9th Jan 3m 5f Mildmay Memorial Handicap Chase, Sandown Park
4th Race	19th Feb 3m Harwell (Amateurs Handicap Chase, Newbury	27th Feb 3m Jed Forrest Handicap Chase, Kelso
5th Race	17th Mar 3m Royal Procelain Handicap Chase, Worcester	Mar Grand National
6th Race	Mar Grand National	

We can, I think, deduce from these two lists that it has been proved a good idea to start the campaign in mid-October, have a second and third race in mid-November and late December/early January respectively. A fourth race in the latter half of February and then in Jay Trump's case have a final preparatory race ten days before the National, whereas Freddie was given a complete month's rest from racing before the Aintree contest. Personally, as you are a permit holder with only limited gallops I am in favour of you following Jay Trump's example and having your fifth race about ten days, but not less, before the National, and don't make it too high class a race like the Cheltenham Gold Cup. Certainly Golden Miller won both the Gold Cup and the National, but keep your main aim in mind which is the National. You do not want to travel much more than 150 miles from your stables so I suggest you go through the *Races to Come* book for the coming season and pick your races accordingly.

I am a strong supporter of the theory, 'horses for courses'. With some of my own horses I have found this to be the

108

case, for instance Waking could always be guaranteed to
run a good race at Plumpton (see plate 10 page 65), and
Le Voyageur, certainly when I had him, took a great liking
to Wincanton and in the first six weeks after Christmas
1957 won what, at today's prize money, amounted to £1,512.
So if you found that Gosford Lad ran very well at any
particular course, during his Novice or Hunterchase engagements, enter him in a three mile handicap race at that
course again.

I would like to see you include the Mildmay Memorial
'chase, if possible, because I am sure that that late West
Country enthusiastic amateur, Lord Mildmay would have
liked to see this Trophy taken back to Devon by an
amateur.

I do not have much to say about Aintree itself except to
say that it would be very *wrong* to try to school him over
any bigger jumps than you already have at Gosford House.
I am enclosing as a postscript to this letter extracts from
an article I wrote for my regimental magazine after my
only appearance at Aintree which may amuse you.

In it you will note that I state that the quarter mile run
from the start to the first jump is a great blessing. I know
that several knowledgeable people will dispute this and tell
you that the reason why so many horses fall at the first
fence is because, with such a long run there is a temptation
to set off at a cracking pace and, consequently, be unbalanced when the jump is reached. I agree that this may
sometimes be the cause of trouble, but I believe that in
most cases a horse falls at the first fence in the National because he is not expecting the slight drop which exists on
the landing side. But on a good jumper, providing that you
do not go at a ridiculously fast pace, and if you sit tight in
case Gosford Lad pecks, you should have nothing to worry
about. Certainly, if I had been able to make the weight to
ride Chamarette in the 1968 National, my tactics would
have been to get out in front, clear of trouble, and stay
there!

I think that there is far more danger of being interfered with by loose horses than there is of going to fast at the first fence. But then, I am probably prejudiced having been put out of the 1957 National by a loose horse.

I hope that your long term plan and determination to win will be well rewarded, but win or lose, I am sure you will agree that your ill luck with Gosford Lass nine years ago has been more than compensated for by the fun you have already had with Gosford Lad.

It only remains for me to wish you the very best of luck on the great day and may your dedication be justly rewarded.

Have fun and enjoy yourself at Aintree.

From,

T.P.

THE GRAND NATIONAL, 1957

P.S.

The Royal Family are once again taking a keen and active interest in steeplechasing, and it is sad to recall the tragedy of last year's National, when the Queen Mother's 'chaser, Devon Loch, with the National apparently well within his reach, faltered and fell on the flat in the final run-in, only a matter of yards from the winning post itself. The cause of his fall will never be known, but without wishing to detract in any way from the fine performance of the winner E.S.B., Devon Loch must surely be one of the unluckiest losers of all time. Let us hope it will not be many years before we once again have a Royal victory in this great race.

The 1936 National provides another heart-rending story – Davy Jones, ridden by the popular amateur,

Lord Mildmay, had a comfortable lead when approaching the last fence, but, also, the buckle of his reins broke and Davy Jones ran out down the wrong course.

But the National is a race in which luck has, and always will, play a decisive part. In my own case, my mount Waking was given the following comment in the *Sporting Life*: 'Waking was put out of the race at the fifth fence by two loose horses, who converged on him, leaving him lying on top of the fence itself!

... I have often been asked what it felt like playing a part in a sporting event of such world-wide interest. Let me recall my memories of that, for me, red-letter day. Many jockeys stay in Liverpool itself, but I was advised, and I think it a pleasanter alternative, to find lodgings near the course. It is quieter, more convenient from the point of view of riding early morning work – and of course, less expensive. The rooms I occupied were ones from which three jockeys had gone out to win the National, the most recent being nineteen years ago, when, in 1938, Bruce Hobbs went out to win on the American-bred gelding, Battleship. This year, four other professional riders shared the rooms with me, and our landlady must have wondered which one of us would bring her tally up to four! But it was not to be; not one of us completed the course, though Derek Ancil went close to winning on Athenian – his mount falling three fences out when practically alongside Sundew and going much the better of the two. The other three rival jockeys sharing my lodgings were Rex Hamey (Monkey Wrench), whose father had won in 1932 on Forvra, Bill Rees (the *Daily Sketch* horse Felias), and David Nicholson (Irish Lizard). David Nicholson's father (the ex-jockey and now Cheltenham trainer, 'Frenchy' Nicholson), was also staying there, and he told me that he had attempted the National seven times, but had never succeeded in completing the course – it was not, as he put it, his lucky course. David, his son, was having, like me, his first National ride, but, I am afraid, he fared no better than his father before him, Becher's Brook claiming his mount, the old stager, Irish Lizard, the first time round.

On the National morning, 'Frenchy' Nicholson woke us with his booming voice, in true Sergeant Major style, at 6.30 – we were due 'on parade' at varying times between 7.15 and 8.00 a.m. to give our mounts a final early morning canter. Jack Barratt, my trainer, had asked me to be there early, before the main body, as he did not want to upset Waking, the old horse being a bit temperamental on such occasions. I was one of the first National entries to be seen out, though several runners in the lesser races were out and about. Waking himself had been fed at six, and was groomed and saddled when I arrived at 7.15 a.m.

Out on the course, the working horses go round the inside track, and I teamed up with a flat racer, whose rider agreed to give me a lead when we swung into the straight and came along the stretch lying parallel to the awe-inspiring 'Chair' fence and water jump. I had been told not to let Waking stride along too fast in his morning work and, as I pulled up, my trainer came running towards me to re-assure himself that all was well. All was, indeed, well and I felt that that added a fillip of confidence which only the impression of well-being and keenness from the horse one is riding can impart.

As I had never seen the National fences, I decided that now was the time to walk the course before the crowds began to gather, and before the atmosphere became overpoweringly charged with anticipation.

I find that riding a fancied horse in any race is a considerable strain. The week before, at Sandown Park, as the Grand Military Meeting approached, the strain had undoubtedly begun to worry me, but now

at Aintree, it was quite different. I knew that not even
my most loyal supporters really expected me to win –
I had, in fact, nothing to lose and could enjoy to the
full the exhilaration that only riding a fit 'chaser over
big fences can give. I will not describe the National
course in detail, but a few points which struck me
most as I walked round are worth noting.

Firstly, there is a run of nearly half a mile to the
first fence, which, in a race such as the National, with
its large number of starters, is a great blessing, as it
enables the field to sort itself out by the time the
fence is reached. The fences vary in height and have
mostly drops on the landing side, but this I did not
find so worrying as the fact that they were nearly all
upright*' which would inevitably provide the added
hazard of one's mount getting too close before taking
off. However, I was cheered by the fact that the fences
were much wider than is the case elsewhere, and that
they stretched right across the course, which not only
meant less of a scrummage, but had the moral advantage of making them look lower than they, in fact,
were. 'Becher's' I found not as awe-inspiring as I had
been led to believe. It is true there was a very big drop
in the landing side of over six feet, but, as Dave Dick,
the 1956 winning rider of E.S.B. remarked to me,
'Don't look down, and you won't get giddy!'. (See
plate 12 page 65.)

The 'Chair' fence is undoubtedly the most awe-
inspiring of all, particularly when viewed from one's
flat feet. It consists of a big open ditch on the take-
off side, which looks like a small chasm, to a five foot
two inch spruce fence, which stands up against the sky
line, tall and forbidding, and looking as formidable as
the Iron Curtain in Berlin. Strangely enough, however,
probably because there is no drop on the landing side,

* The Aintree fences have been modified since 1957. They are now
sloping on the take-off side and very much more inviting.

113

Following next after the 'Chair' is the water jump, which is five yards wide from the take off to landing.

On completing my inspection of the course, I returned to my rooms for breakfast. I had been dieting for the previous three months to get my weight down to nine and a half stone, and did not normally eat breakfast, but 'Frenchy' Nicholson persuaded me to have a little more substantial breakfast than had been my original plan. As he so wisely said, a good breakfast is a sound basis and it provides a reserve power upon which nervous and physical energy can draw. If, as he said, a rider is weak from wasting and unable to ride a strong finish at the end of four and a half miles, he may well handicap the horse far more than the odd pound which he has lost in weight. After breakfast, the morning passed slowly. The others played card, but I am no gambler and preferred to watch. At about one o'clock we left our lodgings for the course. I found it difficult to realise that I was about to play a small part on the main stage of this sporting drama. The crowd recognised some of my companions, and an awed hush fell on them, their expressions signifying a mixture of wonder and surprise that we should be stupid enough to attempt to ride over the big Aintree fences. Once at the course, however, my illusion of being in a dream vanished – it seemed to bring me back to reality, but, to my surprise, I did not feel nearly as strained as I had expected. It does not follow, though, that the calmer one is before the race, the better one will ride. On the contrary, once one is in the saddle, one's nerves and jitterings always vanish, and I have often ridden best when I am particularly jittery in the dressing-room.

Telegrams almost completely covered the weighing room board. I myself had nearly a dozen, for which I was very grateful – one from a naval officer, which ran, rather appropriately: 'X Turret Keep Firing. comparatively few falls occur at the 'Chair' fence.

114

Best of Luck to you both'. (The Royal Marines tradi-
tionally man 'X' Turret in H.M. Ships).

The National was the third race, but owing to the
large number of runners, and to the fact that there was
a parade before the race, it was necessary to weigh out
in good time and most riders began to get ready before
the first race.

As the time drew nearer, the sense of excitement
and anticipation increased. There was the same feeling
of comradeship among the jockeys that arises among
people who share a common danger, however remote
and slight that risk may be. And so the minutes
gradually slipped away, until at last an official
announced 'Jockeys out, please,' and the jockeys
streamed out of the weighing room towards the paddock. Soon, we were mounted, and the drama had
really started. No more stress and strain; nothing to
worry about except the task in hand. On leaving the
paddock, the horses assembled by the gate leading on
to the course and sorted themselves out into the order
in which they appeared on the race card. We then
paraded in single file down the course, with the huge,
tightly packed crowd in the stands on our left, and, on
our right, a thinner gathering spread out along the
rails. It was a great thrill and a very moving experience. When about level with Tattersall's enclosure,
we turned around and cantered slowly back past the
stands.

It was not long now before we were off. As Waking
is a slow beginner, I did not hustle him before the first
fence, and he jumped at the rear of the bunch, but by
no means last. I was advised to sit tight over the first
fence; since Waking had not been to Aintree before,
he would not be prepared for the drop. In the event, he
jumped it very cleanly and could not have given me a
safer first jump. The first fence is never the happiest
stage of a race, and in the National it has the added

uncertainty of how one's horse is going to cope with the drop. Once over, I remember feeling conscious of a considerable sense of relief (see plate 11 page 65). However, no sooner was I over it than I nearly ran into danger. Virginious, who had jumped the fence immediately to my front, appeared to land perfectly, but then seemed to stumble on to his knees and roll over. I had always feared being brought down at the first fence, but Waking was quicker than me and swerving swiftly to his left, the danger was passed almost before I had realised it was there, thanks entirely to Waking's quick reactions.

By the time we had reached the second fence, the field had begun to string out, Armorial being well clear out in front.

The third fence is the first open ditch, and it is advisable to be prepared for a mistake on landing, as the ditch makes horses stand well back, and this, combined with the considerable drop on the landing side, is inclined to make horses land at a steeper angle than is customary. Waking Cleared the fence, but was inclined to jump too big and carefully; rather as if we were show jumping. I think the size of the fences may have had a steadying influence on him, and one of the lessons I learned from this race was that at Aintree, more than at any other course, it is necessary to urge one's mount on with the calves of one's legs to ensure that he maintains his impetus and is kept up into his bridle, and one must give him the full freedom of his head and neck as he lands. I myself have great difficulty in slipping my reins in mid-air – perhaps because my hands are small, and in order to avoid being pulled over Waking's head if he pitched and pecked on landing, particularly at Becher's Brook, I had had a special pair of narrow reins made for the occasion, which, instead of being rubber covered on both sides, only had rubber strips sewn on the outside. I was thus able to get a grip of the rubber between the thumb and fore-finger, but in an emergency I had only to open my fingers and the smooth leather on the inside slipped easily through my hands.

But, to continue the race; at the fourth fence, Armorial could not accommodate himself to the drop and came down heavily, injuring Johnny Bullock, his rider. Armorial himself, however, as I was soon to find to my cost, was unhurt, and was quickly on his feet and galloped off just in front of me, followed closely by a big chestnut, Hart Royal, I think, who had fallen at the first. As we approached the fifth fence, Armorial was in front of Hart Royal, with Waking seven or eight lengths behind. The fence itself is a plain gorse upright fence, five feet high. Armorial, presumably remembering his fall at the fourth, refused: Hart Royal cannoned into him and swerved off to the right, going parallel to the fence itself, and, alas, crossing immediately in front of me at the critical moment when I should have been taking off. Waking was brought practically to a halt and slivered into the foot of the fence, which he gallantly attempted to jump almost from a standstill; but it was no good, he had lost his forward momentum and was only able to leap upwards and landed literally on top of the fence, with his forelegs dangling down on the landing side and his hindlegs on the take-off side. I thus found myself on top of my horse, who in turn was on top of the fence! And so ended my 1957 National venture! Once the field had passed the second time round, we made our way back on the inside of the course and arrived just in time to greet and congratulate Fred Winter as he pulled up Sundew after his great win – everyone was pleased that the popular champion jockey had had his first National win – indeed his first win over the Aintree fences. Of the thirty-five starters, eleven successfully complete the course.

Soon once again we were all in the dressing-room. The room was full of chatter, and Fred Winter quickly produced a crate of champagne, which he generously distributed to his fellow jockeys, the valets, and many others.

I think perhaps my most vivid memory of the 1957 National was the sharp tingle of anticipation in the pit of my stomach as I approached the first fence. A tingle which was replaced by an immediate glow of exhilaration as my gallant Waking cleared the fence and galloped on without a check.

And so I end this series of letters by reminding you how I began in chapter 1 – 'Dedication is the Secret of Successful Steeplechasing.

T.P.

SUMMARY

1. Wrap horses up in cotton wool in the stables, but ride them into the ground on the racecourse. If they are eating up their feed, don't be afraid of running them frequently for two or three weeks and then giving them a rest. A change, such as a days hunting is as good as a rest.
2. Programme of racing engagements in preparation for the Grand National.
3. 'Horses for Courses'.
4. The Grand National, 1957.
5. Dedication is the secret of successful steeplechasing.

Index

muscle development for, 59
race-day routine, 54–7
racing plates, 54
racing seat, 58, 61, 65
starting, 60, 61
See also falling, jumping
Rees, Bill, 111
Rock Salt Lick, 37

Schooling, 73–4, 86–93
  backing, 73, 89, 90
  'bitting' phase, 87–8, 89
  dressage, 94, 97, 98
  jumping, 92, 94
    fences, 99–102
  lead in hand, 73
  long reining, 73, 88, 89
  loose schooling, 73
  lungeing, 29, 73, 87, 89
  mounted schooling, 73
  mounting, 90
  putting to the aids, 90–1
  shoulder-in exercises, 95, 96
scouring, 39
'scrubbing', 64–5
Scudamore, Michael, 100

sex, consideration when buying, 23–4
shoulders, inspection when buying, 21–2
sinus trouble, 50
Sporting Life, The, 20
stable management, 32–43
  ideal routine, 33–4
strapping, 35, 39, 40–1, 52
teeth, 32
training, 44–8
  exercise, 44
  uphill gallop, 45, 46

United Humanitarian League, 30

walking exercise, 29, 35, 44
water, 39
Weatherby's 80, 81
  Regulations, 79, 84
Winter, Fred, 38, 62, 117, 118
withers, inspection when buying, 21–2
worms, 28, 32, 41